The Meaning of Love

Edited by

Phyllis Hobe

A. J. Holman Company

Division of J. B. Lippincott Company

Philadelphia & New York

Printed in the United States of America

*All photographs from Shostal Associates, Inc.
New York*

Photographer's credits by page number

Page 33, H. Foote; 34, W. Hamilton; 51, S. Avery; 52, G. and M. Lincoln; 85, Augusts Upitis; 86, R. F. Head; 119, N. Deak; 120, N. and M. Jansen; 153, D. Dietrich; 154, H. Morton; 171, E. Cooper; 172, G. and M. Lincoln.

U.S. Library of Congress Cataloging in Publication Data

Main entry under title:

The Meaning of love.

Includes index.
1. Love—Literary collections.   2. Love—Quotations, maxims, etc.   I. Hobe, Phyllis.
PN6071.L7M4   808.8'0354   76–23415
ISBN–0–87981–064–5

To John,
who knows the meaning...

Contents

Preface   9

LOVE IS . . .

Joy	13	Romance	84
A memory	17	Excitement	92
Adoration	20	Tranquillity	95
Friendship	24	Kind	99
Wisdom	27	Faith	102
Generous	31	Beauty	107
Courageous	43	Sensitivity	112
A family	45	Noble	115
Contentment	56	A tear	134
Truth	62	Sweetness	140
Forgiveness	64	Considerate	159
Hopeful	72	Everything	168
A place	74	Eternity	183
A sacrifice	76	Divine	190
A dream	83		

Indexes   195

Preface

"My dear," said a friend who is very wise in years, "the trouble with trying to define love is that no one really understands what love is! Only God knows that."

And I realized, after months of collecting statements, thoughts and expressions about love, that she was absolutely correct.

Love is perhaps the most used, least comprehended word in human language. We use it lightly, seriously, sometimes desperately, but not accurately, because the meaning of love is still beyond our grasp. Whether we rejoice because we have found love or weep because we have lost it, love itself always seems to be more than we can possibly imagine. Each of us experiences it in a different way.

In the following pages many men and women describe their individual experiences of love. Some of their words will seem new and delightful as they illuminate some aspect of love which the reader has never known. Others will be warmly familiar because—"Yes, that is how *I* felt!" And, hopefully, love itself will become that much better known and understood.

As for the final, all-encompassing definition of love—indeed, only God can tell us what it really is. And he has already done that, in the person of his Son.

Phyllis Hobe

9

The Meaning of Love

Joy

At the touch of love every one becomes a poet.

Plato

There is nothing holier, in this life of ours, than the first consciousness of love—the first fluttering of its silken wings.

Henry Wadsworth Longfellow

A happy man or woman is a better thing to find than a five-pound note. He or she is a radiating focus of good-will; and their entrance into a room is as though another candle had been lighted. We need not care whether they could prove the forty-seventh proposition; they do a better thing than that—they practically demonstrate the great Theorem of the Livableness of Life.

Robert Louis Stevenson

THE CARE AND FEEDING OF GRANDPARENTS *

In the two years I've been a grandmother, I've learned volumes about living in the kingdom of God. Mary Elizabeth is able to slip up on my blind side with her teaching since she bears no resemblance to a prophet or dominie. Large, round blue eyes and a piquant nose are framed by blond hair like her mother Edith's. At two, she has sturdy, well-formed legs that carry her into the most unlikely places, a disarming smile with a touch of coyness, and a way of pronouncing "yes" and "NO" that makes her sound like a charter member of the Women's Liberation Movement.

What this child does to our household is remarkable. My writing schedule is forgotten while Mary Elizabeth and I enjoy a tea party, using tiny blue china cups acquired just for this occasion. Jeffrey, age fifteen, has no objection to becoming a baby tender. He never walks Mary Elizabeth around the block in her stroller; he races her while she chortles. And you should just see her flirting with the executive editor of *Guideposts*—or better, see him drop down on all fours to bray like a donkey and kick his heels in the air.

All of this adds up to joy. We watch Mary Elizabeth awaken each morning to a world full of wonders. What has become commonplace to us jaded adults still has the freshness of surprise for her. The flying birds, the cloud formations, cows seen in a field, a flower, fragrances, food over which to smack the lips, the rhythm of nursery rhymes and poetry, music—all fill her with excitement.

And like any normal child, she expresses what she feels immediately, exuberantly, without self-consciousness. Her rag doll Muffin had lost her painted-on eyes, nose and mouth in the washing machine. While Mary Elizabeth slept one night, I replaced Muffin's missing features. When this little girl woke to find that Muffin again had a face, she kissed the doll's new eyes over and over in an ecstasy of recognition —while I marveled, not at her open delight, but at my own restraint. How often I too, have felt my heart jump for joy at the sight of a well-loved face after an absence. How inadequate my, "It's nice to see you again."

Through Mary Elizabeth I have been reminded of Christ's extraordinary statement, "Except ye become as little children, ye shall

---

not enter into the kingdom of Heaven." I begin to understand why Jesus was careful to specify the diminutive "little children." These very tiny ones are still fresh from the hand of their Maker, children who have not yet had time to absorb the prejudices, resentments, social distinctions and cruelties we grown-ups mistakenly call "wisdom."

In my reading recently, I have come across descriptions of how adults feel when they enter the kingdom of God through what Jesus called "the new birth." Interestingly, what they experience is almost identical with what we watch in Mary Elizabeth. This is how one woman describes it:

"I cannot say exactly what the mysterious change was. I saw no new thing, but I saw all the usual things in a miraculous new light, in what I believe is their true light. Every human being, every sparrow that flew, every branch tossing in the wind, was caught in and was a part of the whole mad ecstasy of loveliness, of joy, of importance, of intoxication of life. . . ." (Margaret Montague in *Twenty Minutes of Reality*.)

It made me think of Mary Elizabeth's father, Peter John Marshall, at age five, standing with his nose pressed against the windowpane, laughing with glee at the fireworks of an autumn thunderstorm. "Mommy," he said, "the lightning looks like string beans dancing."

Another aspect of this springtime of life—almost as if small children were back in the Garden of Eden—is that Mary Elizabeth feels the necessity of naming every living creature around her. She was not really at home during her first visit to our Florida setting until she had .decided upon names acceptable to her. Thus Mary, who helps us keep house, became "Yehh-yehh"—usually enunciated as lustily as if Mary Elizabeth were rooting for the Braves. Great-grandmother (the original Christy) is tagged "Na-na." I am invariably "My-grandma." Len is "Popi." Last Christmas before Mary Elizabeth could manage two-syllable words, Jesus became "Baby Zoohpff," and I believe that He heartily approves.

Oddly, this naming task was one of the first functions that God gave to the original man Adam. "The Lord God formed every beast of the field and every bird of the air, and brought them to the man to see what he would call them" (Genesis 2:19, RSV).

Another reality of Eden was tender love among living things. We grown-ups have only to watch little children to realize how callused we have become.

Among Mary Elizabeth's favorite books is one of the nursery rhymes set to music. One day her mother sang to her,

"Rock-a-bye baby in the treetop
When the wind blows the cradle will rock.
When the bough breaks the cradle will fall
And down will come baby, cradle and all."

Edith was startled to have her daughter burst into tears. Then she understood: Mary Elizabeth was crying because the baby had fallen down. Since the tears were genuine, Edith made a story of how daddy had come and had picked up the baby, kissed her, and that the baby was not really hurt at all. That comforted Mary Elizabeth temporarily. But from that day to this, whenever she comes to that page of the book, there is a loud "no!" as she flips over the page.

Nor does the little child have any problem about belief in God. These small ones are still living on the border line of two worlds. "Train up a child in the way he should go and when he is old, he will not depart from it," goes the old proverb. Since Jesus said, "I am the way," I am grateful that already our granddaughter is being taught about Him. She doesn't feel happy about going to sleep at night until she shuts her eyes tightly, holds hands with whomever is putting her to bed and says a happy goodnight to the "Baby Zoohpff."

There was a time when we decided it would be less conspicuous simply to murmur a silent grace while dining out in restaurants. Mary Elizabeth speedily changed that. One night when eight of us were seated at a large round table in the very center of a local restaurant, Mary Elizabeth waited till the food was brought, then shut her eyes tightly, bowed her head and held out both her hands for the thank-you. And so we had our family grace, holding hands and all, while Jeff said the prayer in the suddenly very quiet room.

The Kingdom of God! A realm of love and spontaneity and un-abashed delight in God and the wondrous world He made. Jesus told us, "Feed my lambs." This means that we are under orders from Him to give our children the best that we know of His love and under-standing. But one little girl has made me wonder if, after all, we are not the ones who get the feeding.

Catherine Marshall

A memory

TIME LONG PAST

Like the ghost of a dear friend dead
   Is Time long past
A tone which is now forever fled,
A hope which is now forever past,
A love so sweet it could not last,
   Was Time long past.

There were sweet dreams in the night
   Of Time long past.
And, was it sadness or delight,
Each day a shadow onward cast
Which made us wish it yet might last—
   That Time long past.

There is regret, almost remorse,
   For Time long past.
'Tis like a child's beloved corse
A father watches, till at last
Beauty is like remembrance cast
   From Time long past.

Percy Bysshe Shelley

SHE DWELT AMONG THE UNTRODDEN WAYS

She dwelt among the untrodden ways
  Beside the springs of Dove,
A Maid whom there were none to praise
  And very few to love:

A violet by a mossy stone
  Half hidden from the eye!
—Fair as a star, when only one
  Is shining in the sky.

She lived unknown, and few could know
  When Lucy ceased to be;
But she is in her grave, and, oh,
  The difference to me!
                    William Wordsworth

How long it is since she with whom I lay,
Oh Lord, has left for thine my widowed bed;
Yet still our spirits mingle, as our clay,
And she half living yet, and I half dead.
                    Victor Hugo

The present joys of life we doubly taste by looking back with pleasure
on the past.
                    Martial

The heart hath its own memory, like the mind
  And in it are enshrined
The precious keepsakes, into which is wrought
  The giver's loving thought.
                    Henry Wadsworth Longfellow

18

NO TIME LIKE THE OLD TIME

There is no time like the old time, when you and I were young,
When the buds of April blossomed, and the birds of spring-time sung!
The garden's brightest glories by summer suns are nursed,
But on, the sweet, sweet violets, the flowers that opened first!

There is no place like the old place, where you and I were born,
Where we lifted first our eyelids on the splendors of the morn
From the milk-white breast that warmed us, from the clinging arms
   that bore,
Where the dear eyes glistened o'er us that will look on us no more!

There is no friend like the old friend, who has shared our morning days,
No greeting like his welcome, no homage like his praise:
Fame is the scentless sunflower, with gaudy crown of gold;
But friendship is the breathing rose, with sweets in every fold.

There is no love like the old love, that we courted in our pride;
Though our leaves are falling, falling, and we're fading side by side,
There are blossoms all around us with the colors of our dawn,
And we live in borrowed sunshine when the day-star is withdrawn.

There are no times like the old times, —they shall never be forgot!
There is no place like the old place, —keep green the dear old spot!
There are no friends like our old friends, —may Heaven prolong
   their lives!
There are no loves like our old loves—God bless our loving wives!

Oliver Wendell Holmes

Adoration

Praise the Lord!
Praise God in his sanctuary;
  praise him in his mighty firmament!
Praise him for his mighty deeds;
  praise him according to his exceeding greatness!

Praise him with trumpet sound;
  praise him with lute and harp!
Praise him with timbrel and dance;
  praise him with strings and pipe!
Praise him with sounding cymbals;
  praise him with loud clashing cymbals!
Let everything that breathes praise the Lord!
Praise the Lord!
      Psalm 150, Revised Standard Version

TO A BIRD AFTER A STORM

Hither thou com'st: the busy wind all night
Blew through thy lodging, where thine own warm wing
Thy pillow was. Many a sullen storm,
For which course man seems much the fitter born,
    Rain'd on thy bed
    And harmless head.

And now as fresh and cheerful as the light
Thy little heart in early hymns doth sing
Unto that Providence, Whose unseen arm
Curb'd them, and cloth'd thee well and warm.
    All things that be praise Him, and had
    Their lesson taught them when first made.

So hills and valleys into singing break;
And though poor stones have neither speech nor tongue,
While active winds and streams both run and speak,
Yet stones are deep in admiration.
    Thus praise and prayer here beneath the sun
    Make lesser mornings, when the great are done.

Henry Vaughan

NO FAVOR DO I SEEK TODAY

I come not to ASK, to PLEAD or IMPLORE You,
I just come to tell you HOW MUCH I ADORE You,
For to kneel in Your Presence makes me feel blest
For I know that You know all my needs best. . . .
And it fills me with joy just to linger with You
As my soul You replenish and my heart You renew,
For prayer is much more than just asking for things—
It's the PEACE and CONTENTMENT that QUIETNESS brings. . . .
So thank You again for Your MERCY and LOVE
And for making me heir to YOUR KINGDOM ABOVE!

Helen Steiner Rice

We must know before we can love. In order to know God, we must often think of Him; and when we come to love Him, we shall also think of Him often, for our heart will be with our treasure.

Brother Lawrence

In a world where
  there is so much to ruffle the spirit, how needful that
  entering into the secret of God's pavilion, which will
  alone bring it back to composure and peace!
In a world where
  there is so much to sadden and depress, how blessed
  the communion with Him in whom is the one true
  source and fountain of all true gladness and abiding joy!
In a world where
  so much is ever seeking to unhallow our spirits, to
  render them common and profane, how high the
  privilege of consecrating them anew in prayer to
  holiness and to God.

Archbishop Richard Chenevix Trench

BY THE SEA

It is a beauteous evening, calm and free;
The holy time is quiet as a Nun
Breathless with adoration; the broad sun
Is sinking down in its tranquillity;
The gentleness of heaven broods o'er the Sea:
Listen! the mighty Being is awake,
And doth with his eternal motion make
A sound like thunder—everlastingly.
Dear Child! dear Girl! that walkest with me here,
If thou appear untouch'd by solemn thought
Thy nature is not therefore less divine:
Thou liest in Abraham's bosom all the year,
And worshipp'st at the Temple's inner shrine,
God being with thee when we know it not.

William Wordsworth

22

Be silent, O all flesh, before the Lord: for he is raised up out of his holy habitation.

Zechariah 2:13, King James Version

If thou wouldst learn, not knowing how to pray,
Add but a faith, and say as beggars say:
"Master, I'm poor, and blind, in great distress,
Hungry, and lame, and cold and comfortless;
Oh succour him that's grovell'd on the shelf
Of pain, and want, and cannot help himself;
Cast down thine eye upon a wretch, and take
Some pity on me, for sweet Jesus' sake";
But hold! take heed this clause be not put in,
"I never begged before, nor will again."

Francis Quarles

Friendship

I SAW IN LOUISIANA A LIVE-OAK GROWING

I saw in Louisiana a live-oak growing,
All alone stood it and the moss hung down from the branches,
Without any companion it grew there uttering joyous leaves of dark
    green,
And its look, rude, unbending, lusty, made me think of myself,
But I wonder'd how it could utter joyous leaves standing alone there
    without its friend near, for I knew I could not,
And I broke off a twig with a certain number of leaves upon it, and
    twined around it a little moss,
And brought it away, and I have placed it in sight in my room,
It is not needed to remind me as of my own dear friends,
(For I believe lately I think of little else than of them,)
Yet it remains to me a curious token, it makes me think of manly love;
For all that, and though the live-oak glistens there in Louisiana solitary
    in a wide flat space,
Uttering joyous leaves all its life without a friend, a lover near,
I know very well I could not.

Walt Whitman

I had no time to hate, because
The grave would hinder me,
And life was not so ample I
Could finish enmity.

Nor had I time to love; but since
Some industry must be,
The little toil of love, I thought,
Was large enough for me.

Emily Dickinson

Not till the sun excludes you do I exclude you, not till the waters refuse to glisten for you and the leaves to rustle for you, do my words refuse to glisten and rustle for you.

Walt Whitman

 So let us love, dear love, live as we ought;
Love is the lesson which the Lord us taught.

Edmund Spenser

The glory of friendship is not the outstretched hand, nor the kindly smile nor the joy of companionship; it is the spirited inspiration that comes to one when he discovers that someone else believes in him and is willing to trust him.

Ralph Waldo Emerson

We cannot tell the precise moment when friendship is formed. As in filling a vessel drop by drop, there is at last a drop which makes it run over; so in a series of kindnesses there is at last one which makes the heart run over.

Samuel Johnson

The comfort of having a friend may be taken away, but not that of having had one.

Seneca

I do not wish to treat friendships daintily, but with roughest courage. When they are real, they are not glass threads or frostwork, but the solidest thing we know.

Ralph Waldo Emerson

I like a Highland friend who will stand by me, not only when I am in the right, but when I am a little in the wrong.

Sir Walter Scott

Friendship improves happiness, and abates misery, by doubling our joy, and dividing our grief.

Joseph Addison

Of all the things which wisdom provides to make life entirely happy, much the greatest is the possession of friendship.

Epicurus

 Thou shalt love thy neighbor as thyself.
Leviticus 19:18, King James Version

Wisdom

Let me not to the marriage of true minds
Admit impediments. Love is not love
Which alters when it alteration finds,
Or bends with the remover to remove:
Oh, no! it is an ever-fixed mark,
That looks on tempests, and is never shaken;
It is the star to every wandering bark,
Whose worth's unknown, although his height be taken.
Love's not Time's fool, though rosy lips and cheeks
Within his bending sickle's compass come:
Love alters not with his brief hours and weeks,
But bears it out even to the edge of doom:
   If this be error and upon me proved,
   I never writ, nor no man ever loved.
William Shakespeare

To be seventy years young is sometimes far more cheerful and hopeful than to be forty years old.
Oliver Wendell Holmes

Springfield, January 2, 1851. —Dear Brother: Your request for eighty dollars I do not think it best to comply with now. At the various times I have helped you a little you have said: "We can get along very well now," but in a short time I find you in the same difficulty again. Now this can only happen through some defect in you. What that defect is I think I know. You are not lazy, and still you are an idler. I doubt whether since I saw you you have done a good, whole day's work in any one day. You do not very much dislike to work, and still you do not work much, merely because it does not seem to you you get enough for it. This habit of uselessly wasting time is the whole difficulty. It is vastly important to you, and still more to your children, that you break the habit. . . .

You are now in need of some money, and what I propose is that you shall go to work, "tooth and nail," for somebody who will give you money for it. Let father and your boys take charge of your things at home, prepare for a crop and make the crop, and you go to work for the best money wages you can get, or in discharge of any debt you owe, and to secure you a fair reward for your labor, I promise you that for every dollar you will get for your labor between this and the 1st of May, either in money, or in your indebtedness, I will then give you one other dollar. By this, if you hire yourself for ten dollars a month, from me you will get ten dollars more, making twenty dollars. . . .

In this I do not mean that you shall go off to St. Louis or the lead mines in Missouri, or the gold mines in California, but I mean for you to go at it for the best wages you can get close to home in Coles county. If you will do this you will soon be out of debt, and, what is better, you will have acquired a habit which will keep you from getting in debt again. But if I should now clear you out of debt, next year you would be just as deep in debt as ever.

You say you would almost give your place in Heaven for seventy or eighty dollars? Then you value your place in Heaven very cheap, for I am sure you can, with the offer I make, get the seventy or eighty dollars for four or five months' work.

You say if I will lend you the money, you will deed me the land, and, if you don't pay the money back, you will deliver possession. Nonsense! If you cannot now live with the land, how will you then live without it?

You have always been kind to me, and I do not mean to be unkind to you. On the contrary, if you but follow my advice, you will find it worth eighty times eighty dollars to you.

Affectionately your brother,
A. *Lincoln.*

As for a little more money and a little more time, why it's ten to one, if either one or the other would make you one whit happier. If you had more time, it would be sure to hang heavily. It is the working man who is the happy man. Man was made to be active, and he is never so happy as when he is so. It is the idle man who is the miserable man. What comes of holidays, and far too often of sight-seeing, but evil? Half the harm that happens is on those days. And, as for money—Don't you remember the old saying, "Enough is as good as a feast"? Money never made a man happy yet, nor will it. There is nothing in its nature to produce happiness. The more a man has, the more he wants. Instead of its filling a vacuum, it makes one. If it satisfies one want, it doubles and trebles that want another way. That was a true proverb of the wise man, rely upon it: "Better is little with the fear of the Lord, than great treasure, and trouble therewith."

Benjamin Franklin

There never has been, and cannot be, a good life without self-control; apart from self-control, no good life is imaginable. The attainment of goodness must begin with that.

Leo Tolstoy

The supreme happiness of life is the conviction of being loved for yourself, or, more correctly, being loved in spite of yourself.

Victor Hugo

Love of the last word has made more bitterness in families than it is worth. A thousand little differences of this kind would drop to the ground if either party would let them drop. . . . Are they worth ill-tempered words, such as are almost sure to grow out of a discussion? Are they worth throwing away peace and love for? Are they worth the destruction of the only fair ideal left on earth—a quiet, happy home? Better let the most unjust statements pass in silence than risk one's temper in a discussion upon them.

Harriet Beecher Stowe

Endeavor to be always patient of the faults and imperfections of others, for thou hast many faults and imperfections of thy own that require a reciprocation of forbearance. If thou art not able to make thyself that which thou wishest to be, how canst thou expect to mould another in conformity to thy will?

Thomas à Kempis

Our country, right or wrong. When right, to be kept right; when wrong to be put right.

Carl Schurz

All the beautiful sentiments in the world weigh less than a single lovely action.

James Russell Lowell

Generous

Indeed this very love which is my boast,
And which, when rising up from breast to brow,
Doth crown me with a ruby large enow
To draw men's eyes and prove the inner cost,—
This love even, all my worth, to the uttermost,
I should not love withal, unless that thou
Hadst set me an example, shown me how,
When first thine earnest eyes with mine were crossed,
And love called love. And thus, I cannot speak
Of love even, as a good thing of my own:
Thy soul hath snatched up mine all faint and weak,
And placed it by thee on a golden throne,—
And that I love (O soul, we must be meek!)
Is by thee only, whom I love alone.

Elizabeth Barrett Browning

If yet I have not all thy love,
Dear, I shall never have it all,
I cannot breathe one other sigh, to move,
Nor can entreat one other tear to fall,
And all my treasure, which should purchase thee,
Sighs, tears, and oaths, and letters I have spent.
Yet no more can be due to me,
Than at the bargain made was meant;
If then thy gift of love were partial,
That some to me, some should to others fall,
    Dear, I shall never have thee all.

Or if then thou gavest me all,
All was but all, which thou hadst then;
But if in thy heart, since, there be or shall
New love created be, by other men,
Which have their stocks entire, and can in tears,
In sighs, in oaths, and letters outbid me,
This new love may beget new fears,
For, this love was not vowed by thee.
And yet it was, thy gift being general;
The ground, thy heart, is mine, whatever shall
    Grow there, dear, I should have it all.

Yet I would not have all yet;
He that hath all can have no more,
And since my love doth every day admit
New growth, thou shouldst have new rewards in store;
Thou canst not every day give me thy heart,
If thou canst give it, then thou never gavest it:
Love's riddles are, that though thy heart depart,
It stays at home, and thou with losing savest it:
But we will have a way more liberal,
Than changing hearts, to join them, so we shall
    Be one, and one another's all.

John Donne

From LITTLE WOMEN

"November is the most disagreeable month in the whole year," said Margaret, standing at the window one dull afternoon, looking out at the frost-bitten garden.

"That's the reason I was born in it," observed Jo, pensively, quite unconscious of the blot on her nose.

"If something very pleasant should happen now, we should think it a delightful month," said Beth, who took a hopeful view of everything, even November.

"I dare say; but nothing pleasant ever does happen in this family," said Meg, who was out of sorts. "We go grubbing along day after day, without a bit of change, and very little fun. We might as well be in a treadmill."

"My patience, how blue we are!" cried Jo. "I don't much wonder, poor dear, for you see other girls having splendid times, while you grind, grind, year in and year out. Oh, don't I wish I could manage things for you as I do for my heroines! You're pretty enough and good enough already, so I'd have some rich relation leave you a fortune unexpectedly; then you'd dash out as an heiress, scorn everyone who has slighted you, go abroad and come home my Lady Something, in a blaze of splendour and elegance."

"People don't have fortunes left them in that style nowadays; men have to work, and women to marry for money. It's a dreadful unjust world," said Meg, bitterly.

"Jo and I are going to make fortunes for you all; just wait ten years, and see if we don't," said Amy, who sat in a corner, making mud pies, as Hannah called her little clay models of birds, fruits, and faces.

"Can't wait, and I'm afraid I haven't much faith in ink and dirt, though I'm grateful for your good intentions."

Meg sighed, and turned to the frost-bitten garden again; Jo groaned, and leaned both elbows on the table, in a despondent attitude, but Amy patted away energetically; and Beth, who sat at the other window, said, smiling, "Two pleasant things are going to happen right away; Marmee is coming down the street, and Laurie is tramping through the garden as if he had something nice to tell."

In they both came, Mrs. March with her usual question, "Any letter from Father, girls?" and Laurie to say in his persuasive way, "Won't some of you come for a drive? I've been working away at mathematics till my head is in a muddle, and I'm going to freshen my wits by a brisk turn. It's a dull day, but the air isn't bad, and I'm going to take Brooke home, so it will be gay inside, if it isn't out. Come, Jo, you and Beth will go, won't you?"

"Of course we will."

"Much obliged, but I'm busy"; and Meg whisked out her work-basket, for she had agreed with her mother that it was best, for her at least, not to drive often with the young gentleman.

"We three will be ready in a minute," cried Amy, running away to wash her hands.

"Can I do anything for you, Madam Mother?" asked Laurie, leaning over Mrs. March's chair, with the affectionate look and tone he always gave her.

"No, thank you, except call at the office, if you'll be so kind, dear. It's our day for a letter, and the postman hasn't been. Father is as regular as the sun, but there's some delay on the way, perhaps."

A sharp ring interrupted her, and a minute after Hannah came in with a letter.

"It's one of them horrid telegraph things, mum," she said, handing it as if she was afraid it would explode and do some damage.

At the word "telegraph," Mrs. March snatched it, read the two lines it contained, and dropped back into her chair as white as if the little paper had sent a bullet to her heart. Laurie dashed downstairs for water, while Meg and Hannah supported her, and Jo read aloud, in a frightened voice:

"Mrs. March:

Your husband is very ill. Come at once.

S. Hale,

Blank Hospital, Washington."

How still the room was as they listened breathlessly, how strangely the day darkened outside, and how suddenly the whole world seemed to change, as the girls gathered about their mother, feeling as if all the happiness and support of their lives was about to be taken from them. Mrs. March was herself again directly; read the message over, and stretched out her arms to her daughters, saying, in a tone they never forgot, "I shall go at once, but it may be too late. Oh, children, children, help me to bear it!"

For several minutes there was nothing but the sound of sobbing in the room, mingled with broken words of comfort, tender assurances of help, and hopeful whispers that died away in tears. Poor Hannah was the first to recover, and with unconscious wisdom she set all the rest a good example; for, with her, work was the panacea for most afflictions.

"The Lord keep the dear man! I won't waste no time a cryin', but git your things ready right away, mum," she said, heartily, as she wiped her face on her apron, gave her mistress a warm shake of the hand with her own hard one, and went away, to work like three women in one.

"She's right; there's no time for tears now. Be calm, girls, and let me think."

They tried to be calm, poor things, as their mother sat up, looking pale, but steady, and put away her grief to think and plan for them.

"Where's Laurie?" she asked presently, when she had collected her thoughts, and decided on the first duties to be done.

"Here, ma'am. Oh, let me do something!" cried the boy, hurrying from the next room, whither he had withdrawn, feeling that their first sorrow was too sacred for even his friendly eyes to see.

"Send a telegram saying I will come at once. The next train goes early in the morning. I'll take that."

"What else? The horses are ready; I can go anywhere, do anything," he said, looking ready to fly to the ends of the earth.

"Leave a note at Aunt March's. Jo, give me that pen and paper."

Tearing off the blank side of one of her newly-copied pages, Jo drew the table before her mother, well knowing that money for the long, sad journey must be borrowed, and feeling as if she could do anything to add a little to the sum for her father.

"Now go, dear; but don't kill yourself driving at a desperate pace; there is no need of that."

Mrs. March's warning was evidently thrown away; for five minutes later Laurie tore by the window on his own fleet horse, riding as if for his life.

"Jo, run to the rooms, and tell Mrs. King that I can't come. On the way get these things. I'll put them down; they'll be needed, and I must go prepared for nursing. Hospital stores are not always good. Beth, go and ask Mr. Laurence for a couple of bottles of old wine: I'm not too proud to beg for Father; he shall have the best of everything. Amy, tell Hannah to get down the black trunk; and Meg, come and help me find my things, for I'm half bewildered."

Writing, thinking, and directing, all at once, might well bewilder the poor lady, and Meg begged her to sit down quietly in her room for a little while, and let them work. Everyone scattered like leaves before a gust of wind; and the quiet, happy household was broken up as suddenly as if the paper had been an evil spell.

Mr. Laurence came hurrying back with Beth, bringing every comfort the kind old gentleman could think of for the invalid, and friendliest promises of protection for the girls during the mother's absence, which comforted her very much. There was nothing he didn't offer, from his own dressing-gown to himself as escort. But that last was impossible. Mrs. March would not hear of the old gentleman's undertaking the long journey; yet an expression of relief was visible when he spoke of it, for anxiety ill fits one for traveling. He saw the look, knit his heavy eyebrows, rubbed his hands, and marched abruptly away, saying he'd be back directly. No one had time to think of him again till, as Meg ran through the entry, with a pair of rubbers in one hand and a cup of tea in the other, she came suddenly upon Mr. Brooke.

"I'm very sorry to hear of this, Miss March," he said, in the kind, quiet tone which sounded pleasantly to her perturbed spirit. "I came to offer myself as escort to your mother. Mr. Laurence has commissions for me in Washington, and it will give me real satisfaction to be of service to her there."

Down dropped the rubbers, and the tea was very near following, as Meg put out her hand, with a face so full of gratitude, that Mr. Brooke would have felt repaid for a much greater sacrifice than the trifling one of time and comfort which he was about to make.

"How kind you all are! Mother will accept, I'm sure; and it will be such a relief to know that she has someone to take care of her. Thank you very, very much!"

Meg spoke earnestly, and forgot herself entirely, till something in the brown eyes looking down at her made her remember the cooling tea, and lead the way into the parlour, saying she would call her mother.

Everything was arranged by the time Laurie returned with a note from Aunt March enclosing the desired sum, and a few lines repeating what she had often said before—that she had always told them it was absurd for March to go into the army, always predicted that no good would come of it, and she hoped they would take her advice next time. Mrs. March put the note in the fire, the money in her purse, and went on with her preparations, with her lips folded tightly, in a way which Jo would have understood if she had been there.

The short afternoon wore away; all the other errands were done, and Meg and her mother busy at some necessary needlework, while Beth and Amy got tea, and Hannah finished her ironing with what she called a "slap and a bang," but still Jo did not come. They began to get anxious; and Laurie went off to find her, for no one ever knew what freak Jo might take into her head. He missed her, however, and she came walking in with a very queer expression of countenance, for there was a mixture of fun and fear, satisfaction and regret in it, which puzzled the family as much as did the roll of bills she laid before her mother, saying, with a little choke in her voice, "That's my contribution towards making Father comfortable, and bringing him home!"

"My dear, where did you get it? Twenty-five dollars? Jo, I hope you haven't done anything rash?"

"No, it's mine honestly; I didn't beg, borrow, or steal it. I earned it; and I don't think you'll blame me, for I only sold what was my own."

As she spoke, Jo took off her bonnet, and a general outcry arose, for all her abundant hair was cut short.

"Your hair! Your beautiful hair!" "Oh, Jo, how could you? Your one beauty." "My dear girl, there was no need of this." "She doesn't look like my Jo any more, but I love her dearly for it!"

As everyone exclaimed, and Beth hugged the cropped head tenderly, Jo assumed an indifferent air, which did not deceive anyone a particle, and said, rumpling up the brown bush, and trying to look as if she liked it, "It doesn't affect the fate of the nation, so don't wail, Beth. It will be good for my vanity; I was getting too proud of my wig. It will do my brains good to have that mop taken off; my head feels deliciously light and cool, and the barber said I could soon have a curly crop, which will be boyish, becoming, and easy to keep in order. I'm satisfied; so please take the money, and let's have supper."

"Tell me all about it, Jo. I am not quite satisfied, but I can't blame you, for I know how willingly you sacrificed your vanity, as you call it, to your love. But, my dear, it was not necessary, and I'm afraid you will regret it, one of these days," said Mrs. March.

"No, I won't!" returned Jo, stoutly, feeling much relieved that her prank was not entirely condemned.

"What made you do it?" asked Amy, who would as soon have thought of cutting off her head as her pretty hair.

"Well, I was wild to do something for Father," replied Jo, as they gathered about the table, for healthy young people can eat even in the midst of trouble. "I hate to borrow as much as Mother does, and I knew Aunt March would croak; she always does, if you ask for a ninepence. Meg gave all her quarterly salary toward the rent, and I only got some clothes with mine, so I felt wicked, and was bound to have some money, if I sold the nose off my face to get it."

"You needn't feel wicked, my child; you had no winter things, and got the simplest with your own hard earnings," said Mrs. March, with a look that warmed Jo's heart.

"I hadn't the least idea of selling my hair at first, but as I went along I kept thinking what I could do, and feeling as if I'd like to dive into some of the rich stores and help myself. In a barber's window I saw tails of hair with the prices marked; and one black tail, not so thick as mine, was forty dollars. It came over me all of a sudden that I had one thing to make money out of, and without stopping to think, I walked in, asked if they bought hair, and what they would give for mine."

"I don't see how you dared to do it," said Beth, in a tone of awe.

"Oh, he was a little man who looked as if he merely lived to oil his hair. He rather stared, at first, as if he wasn't used to having girls bounce into his shop and ask him to buy their hair. He said he didn't care about mine, it wasn't the fashionable colour, and he never paid much for it in the first place; the work put into it made it dear, and so on. It was getting late, and I was afraid, if it wasn't done right away, that I shouldn't have it done at all, and you know when I start to do a thing, I hate to give it up; so I begged him to take it, and told him why I was in such a hurry. It was silly, I dare say, but it changed his mind, for I got rather excited, and told the story in my topsy-turvy way, and his wife heard, and said so kindly: 'Take it, Thomas, and oblige the young lady; I'd do as much for our Jimmy any day if I had a spire of hair worth selling.'"

"Who was Jimmy?" asked Amy, who liked to have things explained as they went along.

"Her son, she said, who was in the army. How friendly such things make strangers feel, don't they? She talked away all the time the man clipped, and diverted my mind nicely."

"Didn't you feel dreadfully when the first cut came?" asked Meg, with a shiver.

"I took a last look at my hair while the man got his things, and that was the end of it. I never snivel over trifles like that; I will confess, though, I felt queer when I saw the dear old hair laid out on the table, and felt only the short, rough ends on my head. It almost seemed as if I'd an arm or a leg off. The woman saw me look at it, and picked out a long lock for me to keep. I'll give it to you, Marmee, just to remember past glories by; for a crop is so comfortable I don't think I shall ever have a mane again."

Mrs. March folded the wavy chestnut lock, and laid it away with a short grey one in her desk. She only said, "Thank you, deary," but something in her face made the girls change the subject, and talk as cheerfully as they could about Mr. Brooke's kindness, the prospect of a

40

fine day tomorrow, and the happy times they would have when Father came home to be nursed.

No one wanted to go to bed, when, at ten o'clock, Mrs. March put up the last finished job, and said, "Come girls." Beth went to the piano and played the father's favourite hymn; all began bravely, but broke down one by one, till Beth was left alone, singing with all her heart, for to her music was always a sweet consoler.

"Go to bed and don't talk, for we must be up early, and shall need all the sleep we can get. Good night, my darlings," said Mrs. March, as the hymn ended, for no one cared to try another.

They kissed her quietly, and went to bed as silently as if the dear invalid lay in the next room. Beth and Amy soon fell asleep in spite of the great trouble, but Meg lay awake, thinking the most serious thoughts she had ever known in her short life. Jo lay motionless, and her sister fancied that she was asleep, till a stifled sob made her exclaim, as she touched a wet cheek: "Jo, dear, what is it? Are you crying about Father?"

"No, not now."

"What then?"

"My—my hair!" burst out poor Jo, trying vainly to smother her emotion in the pillow.

It did not sound at all comical to Meg, who kissed and caressed the afflicted heroine in the tenderest manner.

"I'm not sorry," protested Jo, with a choke. "I'd do it again tomorrow, if I could. It's only the vain, selfish part of me that goes and cries in this silly way. Don't tell anyone, it's all over now. I thought you were asleep, so I just made a little private moan for my one beauty. How came you to be awake?"

"I can't sleep, I'm so anxious," said Meg.

"Think about something pleasant, and you'll soon drop off."

"I tried it, but felt wider awake than ever."

"What did you think of?"

"Handsome faces—eyes particularly," answered Meg, smiling to herself, in the dark.

"What colour do you like best?"

"Brown—that is, sometimes; blue are lovely."

Jo laughed, and Meg sharply ordered her not to talk, then amiably promised to make her hair curl, and fell asleep to dream of living in her castle in the air.

The clocks were striking midnight, and the rooms were very still, as a figure glided quietly from bed to bed, smoothing a coverlet here, settling a pillow there, and pausing to look long and tenderly at each unconscious face, to kiss each with lips that mutely blessed, and to pray the fervent prayers which only mothers utter. As she lifted the curtain to look out into the dreary night, the moon broke suddenly from behind the clouds, and shone upon her like a bright, benignant face, which seemed to whisper in the silence, "Be comforted, dear soul! There is always light behind the clouds."

Louisa M. Alcott

Courageous

From THE NATURE OF PERSECUTION

The history of persecution is a history of endeavours to cheat nature, to make water run up hill, to twist a rope of sand. It makes no difference whether the actors be many or one, a tyrant or a mob. A mob is a society of bodies voluntarily bereaving themselves of reason, and traversing its work. The mob is man voluntarily descending to the nature of the beast. Its fit hour of activity is night. Its actions are insane like its whole constitution. It persecutes a principle; it would whip a right; it would tar and feather justice, by inflicting fire and outrage upon the houses and persons of those who have these. It resembles the prank of boys, who run with fire-engines to put out the ruddy aurora streaming to the stars. The inviolate spirit turns their spite against the wrongdoers. The martyr cannot be dishonoured. Every lash inflicted is a tongue of fame; every prison, a more illustrious abode; every burned book or house enlightens the world; every suppressed or expunged word reverberates through the earth from side to side.

Ralph Waldo Emerson

SURRENDER

I said, "Let me walk in the field,"
He said: "Nay, walk in the town,"
I said, "There are no flowers there,"
He said: "No flowers, but a crown."

I said, "But the air is thick,
And fogs are veiling the sun."
He said, "Yet souls are sick
And souls in the dark are undone."

I said, "But the skies are black,
There is nothing but noise and din,"
He wept as He sent me back
"There is more," He said, "There is sin."

I said, "I shall miss the light,
And friends will miss me, they say."
He said, "Choose thou tonight
If I am to miss you or they."

I pleaded for time to be given,
He said, "Is it hard to decide?
It will not seem hard in Heaven,
To have followed the steps of your Guide."

I cast one look on the field,
Then turned my face to the town.
He said, "My child, do you yield?
Will you leave the flowers for a crown?"

Then into His hand went mine,
And into my heart came He;
And I walk by a light divine
The path I had feared to see.

George MacDonald

A family

There once lived, in the Government of Ufa, a Bashkir named Elias. His father, who died a year after he had found his son a wife, did not leave him much property. Elias then had only seven mares, two cows, and about a score of sheep. He was a good manager, however, and soon began to acquire more. He and his wife worked from morn till night, rising earlier than others and going later to bed; and his possessions increased year by year. Living in this way, Elias little by little acquired great wealth. At the end of thirty-five years he had 200 horses, 150 head of cattle, and 1,200 sheep. Hired labourers tended his flocks and herds, and hired women milked his mares and cows, and made kumiss, butter, and cheese. Elias had abundance of everything, and every one in the district envied him. They said of him:

"Elias is a fortunate man: he has plenty of everything. This world must be a pleasant place for him."

People of position heard of Elias and sought his acquaintance. Visitors came to him from afar; and he welcomed every one, and gave them food and drink. Whoever might come, there was always kumiss, tea, sherbet, and mutton to set before them. Whenever visitors arrived a sheep would be killed, or sometimes two; and if many guests came he would even slaughter a mare for them.

Elias had three children: two sons and a daughter; and he married them all off. While he was poor, his sons worked with him and looked after the flocks and herds themselves; but when he grew rich they got spoiled, and one of them took to drink. The elder was killed in a brawl; and the younger, who had married a self-willed woman, ceased to obey his father, and they could not live together any more.

So they parted, and Elias gave his son a house and some of the cattle, and this diminished his wealth. Soon after that, a disease broke out among Elias's sheep, and many died. Then followed a bad harvest, and the hay crop failed; and many cattle died that winter. Then the Kirghiz captured his best herd of horses; and Elias's property dwindled away. It became smaller and smaller, while at the same time his strength grew less; till, by the time he was seventy years old, he had begun to sell his furs, carpets, saddles, and tents. At last he had to part with his remaining cattle, and found himself face to face with want. Before he knew how it had happened, he had lost everything, and in their old age he and his wife had to go into service. Elias had nothing left, except the clothes on his back, a fur cloak, a cup, his indoor shoes and over-shoes, and his wife, Sham-Shemagi, who also by this time was old. The son who had parted from him had gone into a far country, and his daughter was dead, so that there was no one to help the old couple.

Their neighbor, Muhammad-Shah, took pity on them. Muhammad-Shah was neither rich nor poor, but lived comfortably, and was a good man. He remembered Elias's hospitality, and, pitying him, said:

"Come and live with me, Elias, you and your old woman. In summer you can work in my melon-garden as much as your strength allows, and in winter feed my cattle; and Sham-Shemagi shall milk my mares and make kumiss. I will feed and clothe you both. When you need anything, tell me, and you shall have it."

Elias thanked his neighbour, and he and his wife took service with Muhammad-Shah as labourers. At first the position seemed hard to them, but they got used to it, and lived on, working as much as their strength allowed.

Muhammad-Shah found it was to his advantage to keep such people, because, having been masters themselves, they knew how to manage and were not lazy, but did all the work they could. Yet it grieved Muhammad-Shah to see people brought so low who had been of such high standing.

It happened once that some of Muhammad-Shah's relatives came from a great distance to visit him, and a Mullah came too. Muhammad-Shah told Elias to catch a sheep and kill it. Elias skinned the sheep and boiled it, and sent it in to the guests. The guests ate the mutton, had some tea, and then began drinking kumiss. As they were sitting with their host on down cushions on a carpet, conversing and sipping kumiss from their cups, Elias, having finished his work, passed by the open door. Muhammad-Shah, seeing him pass, said to one of the guests:

"Did you notice that old man who passed just now?"

"Yes," said the visitor, "what is there remarkable about him?"

"Only this—that he was once the richest man among us," replied the host. "His name is Elias. You may have heard of him."

"Of course I have heard of him," the guest answered. "I never saw him before, but his fame has spread far and wide."

"Yes, and now he has nothing left," said Muhammad-Shah, "and he lives with me as my labourer, and his old woman is here too—she milks the mares."

The guest was astonished: he clucked with his tongue, shook his head, and said:

"Fortune turns like a wheel. One man it lifts, another it sets down! Does not the old man grieve over all he has lost?"

"Who can tell? He lives quietly and peacefully, and works well."

"May I speak to him?" asked the guest. "I should like to ask him about his life."

"Why not?" replied the master, and he called from the kibitka in which they were sitting:

"Babay" (which in the Bashkir tongue means "Grandfather"), "come in and have a cup of kumiss with us, and call your wife here also."

Elias entered with his wife; and after exchanging greetings with his master and the guests, he repeated a prayer and seated himself near the door. His wife passed him behind the curtain and sat down with her mistress.

A cup of kumiss was handed to Elias; he wished the guests and his master good health, bowed, drank a little, and put down the cup.

"Well, Daddy," said the guest who had wished to speak to him, "I suppose you feel rather sad at the sight of us. It must remind you of your former prosperity and of your present sorrows."

Elias smiled, and said:

"If I were to tell you what is happiness and what is misfortune, you would not believe me. You had better ask my wife. She is a woman, and what is in her heart is on her tongue. She will tell you the whole truth."

The guest turned towards the curtain.

"Well, Granny," he cried, "tell me how your former happiness compares with your present misfortune."

And Sham-Shemagi answered from behind the curtain:

"This is what I think about it: My old man and I lived for fifty years seeking happiness and not finding it; and it is only now, these last two years, since we had nothing left and have lived as labourers that we have found real happiness, and we wish for nothing better than our present lot."

The guests were astonished, and so was the master; he even rose and drew the curtain back, so as to see the old woman's face. There she stood with her arms folded, looking at her old husband, and smiling; and he smiled back at her. The old woman went on:

"I speak the truth and do not jest. For half a century we sought for happiness, and as long as we were rich we never found it. Now that we have nothing left and have taken service as labourers, we have found such happiness that we want nothing better."

"But in what does your happiness consist?" asked the guest.

"Why, in this," she replied, "when we were rich, my husband and I had so many cares that we had no time to talk to one another, or to think of our souls, or to pray to God. Now we had visitors, and had to consider what food to set before them, and what presents to give them, lest they should speak ill of us. When they left we had to look after our labourers, who were always trying to shirk work and get the best food, while we wanted to get all we could out of them. So we sinned. Then we were in fear lest a wolf should kill a foal or a calf, or thieves steal our horses. We lay awake at night worrying lest the ewes should overlie their lambs, and we got up again and again to see that all was well. One thing attended to, another care would spring up: how, for instance, to get enough fodder for the winter. And besides that, my old man and I used to disagree. He

48

would say we must do so and so, and I would differ from him; and then we disputed—sinning again. So we passed from one trouble to another, from one sin to another, and found no happiness."

"Well, and now?"

"Now, when my husband and I wake in the morning we always have a loving word for one another, and we live peacefully, having nothing to quarrel about. We have no care but how best to serve our master. We work as much as our strength allows, and do it with a will, that our master may not lose, but profit by us. When we come in, dinner or supper is ready and there is kumiss to drink. We have fuel to burn when it is cold, and we have our fur cloak. And we have time to talk, time to think of our souls, and time to pray. For fifty years we sought happiness, but only now at last have we found it."

The guests laughed.

But Elias said:

"Do not laugh, friends. It is not a matter for jesting—it is the truth of life. We also were foolish at first and wept at the loss of our wealth; but now God has shown us the truth, and we tell it, not for our own consolation, but for your good."

And the Mullah said:

"That is a wise speech. Elias has spoken the exact truth. The same is said in Holy Writ."

And the guests ceased laughing and became thoughtful.

Leo Tolstoy

Lord, behold our family here assembled. We thank Thee for this place in which we dwell; for the love that unites us; for the peace accorded us this day; for the hope with which we expect the morrow; for the health, the work, the food and the bright skies that make our lives delightful; for our friends in all parts of the earth, and our friendly helpers in this foreign isle.

Robert Louis Stevenson

WITH GOD AS YOUR PARTNER

It takes a GROOM,
   it takes a BRIDE,
TWO PEOPLE standing side by side . . .
It takes a RING
   and VOWS that say
This is OUR HAPPY WEDDING DAY. . . .
But marriage vows
   are sanctified
And loving hearts are unified
When standing
   with the bride and groom,
Unseen by others in the room,
The "SPIRIT OF THE LORD" is there
To bless this
   happy bridal pair. . . .
For "GOD IS LOVE," and married life
Is richer for both
   man and wife
When God becomes a partner, too,
In everything
   they plan and do. . . .
And every home
   is specially blest
When God is made a "DAILY GUEST."
For married folks
   who pray together
Are happy folks who stay together. . . .
For when God's love
   becomes a part
Of body, mind, and soul and heart,
Their love becomes
   a wondrous blending
That's both ETERNAL and UNENDING,
And God looks down
   and says "well done" . . .
For now you TWO are truly ONE.

Helen Steiner Rice

You do not know how much I have missed you and the children, my dear Mary. To be alone in a crowd is very solitary. In the woods, I feel sympathy with the trees and birds, in whose company I take delight, but experience no pleasure in a strange crowd. I hope you are all well and will continue so, and, therefore, must again urge you to be very prudent and careful of those dear children. If I could only get a squeeze at that little fellow, turning up his sweet mouth to "keese baba!" You must not let him run wild in my absence, and will have to exercise firm authority over all of them. This will not require severity or even strictness, but constant attention and an unwavering course. Mildness and forbearance will strengthen their affection for you, while it will maintain your control over them.

Robert E. Lee

AS THRO' THE LAND AT EVE WE WENT

As thro' the land at eve we went,
　And pluck'd the ripen'd ears,
We fell out, my wife and I,
O we fell out I know not why,
　And kiss'd again with tears.
And blessings on the falling out
　That all the more endears,
When we fall out with those we love
　And kiss again with tears!
For when we came where lies the child
　We lost in other years,
There above the little grave,
O there above the little grave,
　We kiss'd again with tears.
Alfred, Lord Tennyson

From BABY

Where did you come from, baby dear?
Out of the everywhere into the here.

Where did you get those eyes so blue?
Out of the sky as I came through.

What makes the light in them sparkle and spin?
Some of the starry spikes left in.

Where did you get that little tear?
I found it waiting when I got here.

What makes your forehead so smooth and high?
A soft hand stroked it as I went by.

What makes your cheek like a warm white rose?
I saw something better than any one knows.

Whence that three-cornered smile of bliss?
Three angels gave me at once a kiss.

Where did you get this pearly ear?
God spoke, and it came out to hear.

Where did you get those arms and hands?
Love made itself into bonds and bands.

Feet, whence did you come, you darling things?
From the same box as the cherubs' wings.

How did they all just come to be you?
God thought about me, and so I grew.

But how did you come to us, you dear?
God thought about you, and so I am here.

George MacDonald

54

"Take us the foxes, the little foxes, that spoil the vines, for our vines have tender grapes." . . . "Little foxes," by which I mean those unsuspected, unwatched, insignificant little causes that nibble away domestic happiness, and make home less than so noble an institution should be. You may build beautiful, convenient, attractive houses—you may hang the walls with lovely pictures and stud them with gems of Art; and there may be living there together persons bound by blood and affection in one common interest, leading a life common to themselves and apart from others; and these persons may each of them be possessed of good and noble traits; there may be a common basis of affection, of generosity, of good principle, of religion; and yet, through the influence of some of these perverse, nibbling, insignificant little foxes, half the clusters of happiness on these so promising vines may fail to come to maturity. A little community of people, all of whom may be willing to die for each other, may not be able to live happily together; that is, they may have far less happiness than their circumstances, their fine and excellent traits, entitle them to expect.

The reason for this in general is that home is a place not only of strong affections, but of entire unreserve; it is life's undress rehearsal, its back-room, its dressing-room, from which we go forth to more careful and guarded intercourse, leaving behind us much debris of cast-off and everyday clothing.

Harriet Beecher Stowe

Contentment

SONNET OF CONTENTMENT

To one who has been long in city pent
'Tis very sweet to look into the fair
And open face of heaven, to breathe a prayer
Full in the smile of the blue firmament.
Who is more happy, when, with heart's content,
Fatigued he sinks into some pleasant lair
Of wavy grass, and reads a debonair
And gentle tale of love and languishment?
Returning home at evening, with an ear
Catching the notes of Philomel, and eye
Watching the sailing cloudlet's bright career,
He mourns that day so soon has glided by,
Even like the passage of an angel's tear
That falls through the clear ether silently.

John Keats

Blessed is every one who fears the Lord,
    who walks in his ways!
You shall eat the fruit of the labor of your hands;
    you shall be happy, and it shall be well with you.
Your wife will be like a fruitful vine within your house;
    your children will be like olive shoots around your table.
Psalm 128:1–3, Revised Standard Version

I am content with what I have,
Little be it, or much.
John Bunyan

Let me but live my life from year to year,
    With forward face and unreluctant soul.
    Not hurrying to, nor turning from the goal;
Not mourning for the things that disappear
In the dim past, nor holding back in fear
    From what the future veils; but with a whole
    And happy heart, that pays its toll
To youth and age, and travels on with cheer.
Robert Browning

Cheerfulness means a contented spirit; a pure heart, a kind and loving disposition; it means humility and charity, a generous appreciation of others, and a modest opinion of self.
William Makepeace Thackeray

57

From THE PRACTICE OF THE PRESENCE OF GOD

As for my set hours of prayer, they are only a continuation of the same exercise. Sometimes I consider myself there as a stone before a carver, whereof he is to make a statue; presenting myself thus before God, I desire Him to form His perfect image in my soul, and make me entirely like Himself.

At other times, when I apply myself to prayer, I feel all my spirit and all my soul lift itself up without any care or effort of mine, and it continues as it were suspended and firmly fixed in God, as in its center and place of rest.

I know that some charge this state with inactivity, delusion, and self-love. I confess that it is a holy inactivity, and would be a happy self-love if the soul in that state were capable of it, because, in effect, while she is in this repose, she cannot be disturbed by such acts as she was formerly accustomed to, and which were then her support, but which would now rather hinder than assist her.

Yet I cannot bear that this should be called delusion, because the soul which thus enjoys God desires herein nothing but Him. If this be delusion in me, it belongs to God to remedy it. Let Him do what He pleases with me; I desire only Him, and to be wholly devoted to Him.

Brother Lawrence

Behold, how good and pleasant it is
   when brothers dwell in unity!
It is like the precious oil upon the head,
   running down upon the beard. . . .
It is like the dew of Hermon,
   which falls on the mountains of Zion!
For the Lord has commanded the blessing,
   life for evermore.
   Psalm 133, Revised Standard Version

THE COMPLEAT ANGLER

Oh the brave Fisher's life,
It is the best of any,
'Tis full of pleasure, void of strife,
And 'tis belov'd of many:

       Other joyes
       are but toyes
       only this
       lawful is,
       for our skil
       breeds no ill,
but content and pleasure.
In a morning up we rise
Ere Aurora's peeping,
Drink a cup to wash our eyes,
Leave the sluggard sleeping;
       Then we go
       to and fro,
       with our knacks
       at our backs,
       to such streams
       as the Thames
if we have the leisure.
When we please to walk abroad
For our recreation,
In the fields is our abode,
Full of delectation:
       Where in a Brook
       with a hook,
       or a Lake
       fish we take,
       there we sit
       for a bit,
till we fish intangle.
We have Gentles in a horn,
We have Paste and worms too,
We can watch both night and morn,
Suffer rain and storms too;

                              None do here
                              use to swear,
                              oathes do fray
                              fish away,
                              we sit still,
                              watch our quill,

Fishers must not rangle.
If the Sun's excessive heat
Makes our bodies swelter
To an Osier hedge we get
for a friendly shelter,
                              where in a dike
                              Pearch or Pike,
                              Roch or Dace
                              we do chase
                              Bleak or Gudgion
                              without grudging,
we are still contented.

Or we sometime pass an hour,
Under a green willow,
That defends us from a shower,
Making earth our pillow,
                              There we may
                              think and pray
                              before death
                              stops our breath;
                              other joyes
                              are but toyes
and to be lamented.

Izaak Walton

A STATE OF BLESSEDNESS

I know a lady who has entered into many blissful satisfactions, and recently a friend remarked to her, "Oh, how fortunate you are! You only have to wish for a thing, and it comes to you." And it did, indeed, appear so on the surface; but in reality all the blessedness that has entered into this woman's life is the direct outcome of the inward state of blessedness which she has, throughout life, been cultivating and training toward perfection. Mere wishing brings nothing but disappointment; it is living that tells. The foolish wish and grumble; the wise work and wait. And this woman had worked; worked without and within, but especially within upon heart and soul; and with the invisible hands of the spirit she had built up, with the precious stones of faith, hope, joy, devotion, and love, a fair temple of light, whose glorifying radiance was ever round about her. It beamed in her eye; it shone through her countenance; it vibrated in her voice; and all who came into her presence felt its captivating spell.

And as with her, so with you. Your success, your failure, your influence, your whole life you carry about with you, for your dominant trends of thought are the determining factors in your destiny. Send forth loving, stainless, and happy thoughts, and blessings will fall into your hands, and your table will be spread with the cloth of peace.

James Allen

Truth

And this is especially to be insisted on in the early education of young people. It should be pointed out to them with continual earnestness that the essence of lying is in deception, not in words: a lie may be told by silence, by equivocation, by the accent on a syllable, by a glance of the eye attaching a peculiar significance to a sentence; and all these kinds of lies are worse and baser by many degrees than a lie plainly worded; so that no form of blinded conscience is so far sunk as that which comforts itself for having deceived, because the deception was by gesture or silence, instead of utterance; and finally, according to Tennyson's deep and trenchant line, "A lie which is half a truth is ever the worst of lies."

John Ruskin

There is no playing fast and loose with the truth, in any game, without growing the worse for it.

Charles Dickens

TO KEEP A TRUE LENT

Is this a Fast, to keep
   The larder lean,
     And clean
From fat of veals and sheep?

Is it to quit the dish
   Of flesh, yet still
     To fill
The platter high with fish?

Is it to fast an hour,
   Or ragg'd to go,
     Or show
A downcast look and sour?

NO: 'tis a Fast to dole
   Thy sheaf of wheat
     And meat,
Unto the hungry soul.

It is to fast from strife,
   From old debate
     And hate;
To circumcise thy life.

To show a heart grief-rent;
   To starve thy sin,
     Not bin:
And that's to keep thy Lent.
          Robert Herrick

Forgiveness

GOOD FRIDAY

Am I a stone, and not a sheep,
   That I can stand, O Christ, beneath Thy cross,
   To number drop by drop Thy Blood's slow loss,
And yet not weep?

Not so those women loved
   Who with exceeding grief lamented Thee;
   Not so fallen Peter weeping bitterly;
Not so the thief was moved;

Not so the Sun and Moon
   Which hid their faces in a starless sky.
   A horror of great darkness at broad noon—
I, only I.

Yet give not o'er
   But seek Thy sheep, true Shepherd of the flock;
   Greater than Moses, turn and look once more
And smite a rock.

Christina Rossetti

LOVE BADE ME WELCOME

Love bade me welcome; yet my soul drew back,
  Guilty of dust and sin.
But quick-eyed Love, observing me grow slack
  From my first entrance in,
Drew nearer to me, sweetly questioning
  If I lacked any thing.

"A guest," I answered, "worthy to be here":
  Love said, "You shall be he."
"I the unkind, ungrateful? Ah my dear!
  I cannot look on thee."
Love took my hand, and smiling did reply,
  "Who made the eyes but I?"

"Truth, Lord, but I have marred them: let my shame
  Go where it doth deserve."
"And know you not," says Love, "who bore the blame?"
  "My dear, than I will serve."
"You must sit down," says Love, "and taste my meat."
  So I did sit and eat.

George Herbert

Therefore the Lord himself shall give you a sign;
Behold, a virgin shall conceive,
and bear a son,
and shall call his name Immanuel.
  Isaiah 7:14, King James Version

65

There was once a man who lived for seventy years in the world, and lived in sin all that time. He fell ill, but even then did not repent. Only at the last moment, as he was dying, he wept and said:

"Lord! forgive me, as Thou forgavest the thief upon the cross."

And as he said these words, his soul left his body. And the soul of the sinner, feeling love towards God and faith in His mercy, went to the gates of heaven, and knocked, praying to be let into the heavenly kingdom.

Then a voice spoke from within the gate:

"What man is it that knocks at the gates of Paradise, and what deeds did he do during his life?"

And the voice of the Accuser replied, recounting all the man's evil deeds, and not a single good one.

And the voice from within the gates answered:

"Sinners cannot enter into the kingdom of heaven. Go hence!"

Then the man said:

"Lord, I hear thy voice, but cannot see thy face, nor do I know thy name."

The voice answered:

"I am Peter, the Apostle."

And the sinner replied:

"Have pity on me, Apostle Peter! Remember man's weakness, and God's mercy. Wert not thou a disciple of Christ? Didst not thou hear his teaching from his own lips, and hadst thou not his example before thee? Remember then how, when three times he asked thee to keep awake and pray, thou didst sleep, because thine eyes were heavy, and three times he found thee sleeping. So it was with me. Remember, also, how thou didst promise to be faithful unto death, and yet didst thrice deny him, when he was taken before Caiaphas. So it was with me. And remember, too, how when the cock crowed thou didst go out and didst weep bitterly. So it is with me. Thou canst not refuse to let me in."

And the voice behind the gates was silent.

Then the sinner stood a little while, and again began to knock, and to ask to be let into the kingdom of heaven.

And he heard another voice behind the gates, which said:

"Who is this man, and how did he live on earth?"

And the voice of the Accuser again repeated all the sinner's evil deeds, and not a single good one.

And the voice from behind the gates replied:

"Go hence! Such sinners cannot live with us in Paradise." Then the sinner said:

66

"Lord, I hear thy voice, but I see thee not, nor do I know thy name."

And the voice answered:

"I am David, king and prophet."

The sinner did not despair, nor did he leave the gates of Paradise, but said:

"Have pity on me, King David! Remember man's weakness, and God's mercy. God loved thee and exalted thee among men. Thou hadst all: a kingdom, and honour, and riches, and wives, and children; but thou sawest from thy house-top the wife of a poor man, and sin entered into thee, and thou tookest the wife of Uriah and didst slay him with the sword of the Ammonites. Thou, a rich man, didst take from the poor man his one ewe lamb and didst kill him. I have done likewise. Remember, then, how thou didst repent, and how thou saidst, 'I acknowledge my transgressions: my sin is ever before me.' I have done the same. Thou canst not refuse to let me in."

And the voice from within the gates was silent.

The sinner, having stood a little while, began knocking again, and asking to be let into the kingdom of heaven. And a third voice was heard within the gates, saying:

"Who is this man, and how has he spent his life on earth?"

And the voice of the Accuser replied for the third time, recounting the sinner's evil deeds, and not mentioning one good deed.

And the voice within the gates said:

"Depart hence! Sinners cannot enter into the kingdom of heaven."

And the sinner said:

"Thy voice I hear, but thy face I see not, neither do I know thy name."

Then the voice replied:

"I am John the Divine, the beloved disciple of Christ."

And the sinner rejoiced and said:

"Now surely I shall be allowed to enter. Peter and David must let me in, because thou lovest much. Was it not thou, John the Divine, who wrote that God is Love, and that he who loves not, knows not God? And in thine old age didst thou not say unto men: 'Brethren, love one another?' How, then, canst thou look on me with hatred, and drive me away? Either thou must renounce what thou has said, or loving me, must let me enter the kingdom of heaven."

And the gates of Paradise opened, and John embraced the repentant sinner and took him into the kingdom of heaven.

Leo Tolstoy

If any one is in Christ, he is a new creation; the old has passed away, behold, the new has come. All this is from God, who through Christ reconciled us to himself and gave us the ministry of reconciliation; that is, God was in Christ reconciling the world to himself, not counting their trespasses against them, and entrusting to us the message of reconciliation.

II Corinthians 5:17–19, Revised Standard Version

And Jesus said, "Father, forgive them; for they know not what they do."

Luke 23:34, Revised Standard Version

Batter my heart, three person'd God; for, you
As yet but knock, breathe, shine, and seek to mend;
That I may rise, and stand, o'erthrow me, and bend
Your force, to break, blow, turn and make me new.
I, like an usurpt town, to another due,
Labour to admit you, but Oh, to no end,
Reason your viceroy in me, me should defend,
But is captiv'd, and proves weak or untrue.
Yet dearly 'I love you,' and would be loved fain,
But am betroth'd unto your enemy:
Divorce me, untie, or break that knot again,
Take me to you, imprison me, for I,
Except you enthrall me, never shall be free,
Nor ever chaste, except you ravish me.

John Donne

And when with grief you see your brother stray
Or in a night of error lose his way,
Direct his wandering and restore the day . . .
Leave to avenging Heaven his stubborn will,
For, O, remember, he's your brother still.

Jonathan Swift

A BALLAD OF TREES AND THE MASTER

Into the woods my Master went.
Clean forspent, forspent.
Into the woods my Master came,
Forspent with love and shame.
But the olives they were not blind to Him,
The little gray leaves were kind to Him:
The thorn-tree had a mind to Him
When into the woods He came.

Out of the woods my Master went,
And He was well content.
Out of the woods my Master came,
Content with death and shame.
When Death and Shame would woo Him last,
From under the trees they drew Him last:
'Twas on a tree they slew Him—last
When out of the woods He came.

Sidney Lanier

THE ALL-EMBRACING

There's a wideness in God's mercy,
    Like the wideness of the sea;
There's a kindness in His justice,
    Which is more than liberty.

There is welcome for the sinner,
    And more graces for the good;
There is mercy with the Saviour;
    There is healing in His blood.

For the love of God is broader
    Than the measure of man's mind;
And the heart of the Eternal
    Is most wonderfully kind.

If our love were but more simple,
    We should take Him at His word;
And our lives would be all sunshine
    In the sweetness of our Lord.
                Frederick W. Faber

From THE MERCHANT OF VENICE

The quality of mercy is not strain'd,
It droppeth as the gentle rain from heaven
Upon the place beneath. It is twice bless'd:
It blesseth him that gives and him that takes.
'Tis mightiest in the mightiest: it becomes
The throned monarch better than his crown:
His sceptre shows the force of temporal power,
The attribute to awe and majesty,
Wherein doth sit the dread and fear of kings;
But mercy is above this sceptred sway,
It is enthroned in the hearts of kings,
It is an attribute to God himself;

And earthly power doth then show likest God's,
When mercy seasons justice. Therefore . . .
Though justice by thy plea, consider this—
That in the course of justice none of us
Should see salvation. We do pray for mercy;
And that same prayer doth teach us all to render
The deeds of mercy.

William Shakespeare

Hopeful

You ask if I would agree to live my seventy or rather seventy-three years over again? To which I say yea. I think with you that it is a good world on the whole; that it has been framed on a principle of benevolence, and more pleasure than pain dealt out to us. There are, indeed, (who might say nay) gloomy and hypochondriac minds, inhabitants of diseased bodies, disgusted with the present, and despairing of the future; always counting that the worst will happen, because it may happen. To these I say, how much pain have cost us the evils which have never happened! My temperament is sanguine.

Thomas Jefferson

  Put in the plow
And plant the great hereafter in the now.
Robert Browning

Put thy trust in God,
Let Him be thy fear and thy love.
He shall answer for thee
And will do in all things what is best for thee.
Thomas à Kempis

Ah! What would the world be to us
If the children were no more?
We should dread the desert behind us
Worse than the dark before.
Henry Wadsworth Longfellow

The Lord is the portion of mine inheritance
and of my cup:
thou maintainest my lot.
The lines are fallen unto me in pleasant places;
yea, I have a goodly heritage.
I will bless the Lord, who hath given me counsel:
my reins also instruct me in the night seasons.
therefore my heart is glad,
and my glory rejoiceth:
my flesh also shall rest in hope.
Psalm 16:5, 6, 7, 9, King James Version

A place

Such is the patriot's boast, where'er we roam,
His first, best country ever is at home.

Oliver Goldsmith

From MY HEART'S IN THE HIGHLANDS

Farewell to the Highlands, farewell to the North,
The birth-place of valor, the country of worth!
Wherever I wander, wherever I rove,
The hills of the Highlands for ever I love.

My heart's in the Highlands, my heart is not here,
My heart's in the Highlands a-chasing the deer,
A-chasing the wild deer and following the roe—
My heart's in the Highlands, wherever I go.

Robert Burns

THE WISH OF DIOGENES

A hermit's house beside a stream
With forests planted round,
Whatever it to you may seem
More real happiness I deem
Than if I were a monarch crown'd.
Philip Freneau

PATRIOTISM

Breathes there a man with soul so dead
Who never to himself hath said,
"This is my own, my native land!"
Whose heart hath ne'er within him burned
As home his footsteps he hath turned
From wandering on a foreign strand?
If such there breathe, go, mark him well!
For him no minstrel raptures swell;
High though his titles, power, and pelf,
The wretch, concentred all in self,
Living, shall forfeit fair renown,
And, doubly dying, shall go down
To the vile dust from whence he sprung,
Unwept, unhonored, and unsung.
Sir Walter Scott

A sacrifice

Greater love hath no man than this, that a man lay down his life for his friends.

John 15:13, King James Version

He loved me well;
so well he could but die
To show he loved me better
than his life; he lost it
for me.

John Dryden

He who bestows his goods upon the poor,
Shall have as much again, and ten times more.

John Bunyan

LOVE IS SOMETHING YOU DO *

The other evening we entertained two of our country's most popular singers—via TV. One of them sang that "Love is a many-splendored thing," and he sang it well but he left it more pretty than practical—way up there "on a windy hill," a lonely ghost looking for a place to land. The other warbled a question: "What is this thing called love?" but he didn't get around to answering his own question.

All this had a sweet sound, but it left us feeling cheated. It wasn't enough. Not nearly enough. Love is a lot more than this.

Love is a fire that can either purify or destroy.

Love can lift us up to sing on a mountain-top or it can be as dangerous as dynamite.

Love sometimes is moonlight and roses, but not always; roses have a habit of withering and dying, and astronauts walking on the ball of dirt called "the moon" have robbed it of its old romantic glow.

Love is an idea born in the heart of a God whose other name is love, "a doorway through which the human soul passes from selfishness to service and from solitude to kinship with all mankind."

Love is not so much an emotion as it is an education, and the education starts the minute the doctor says to the panting mother, "You have a fine, healthy baby"—and proceeds to welcome the fine, healthy baby into his new world with a most inhospitable slap. The baby yells; another protester is born.

Now a great deal has been said, written, and sung about the love of the mother and the babe; the Madonna-faced mother with the happy-faced baby in her arms seems to be the perfect picture. We heard a preacher say recently that "To the baby, the mother is God." Maybe so. That's quite a compliment to the mother, if not to God, and it may be good, for at this point all the love is on the mother's side. You could murmur the words "love" and "God" into the baby's ear until you are blue in the face, and he wouldn't have the faintest idea of what you are talking about. A baby is too young for words; he will learn later; right now he cries for his mother not because he loves her but because he is hungry and wants to be fed, or he is tired of his little prison crib and wants to be picked up and cuddled. Feed and cuddle him, and he turns off the tears with the greatest of ease.

He may scream occasionally in fear (fear of a loud noise, or waking up in the darkness of night), but more often he screams to get

* Copyright © 1976 by Frank S. Mead.

77

the comfort he wants and get it quickly. The mother loves him, yes, but the only love you could credit the baby with is a love of self. That's both good and bad: we can hardly learn to love others until we have loved ourselves, but when we know *only* self-love, we are developing a lifestyle that will make others shun us as even his friends shunned Cain. The baby isn't aware of that when he cried for round-the-clock service from his mother and the security of her arms, and so he develops a gimme-game relationship with her. Gimme food. Gimme a little patting on the back. Gimme attention—at 2 A.M.

We smile at the clever little rascal—and then a lot of us pick up the game where he left off and play it all the rest of our lives. Gimme this. Gimme that. Gimme money. Gimme a good job whether I'm qualified for it or not, gimme a nice big house, a Continental, a nice big (the biggest) mausoleum of my own in the cemetery when I die. A quite successful man gave us some advice just a month ago: "Get a good stack of money in the bank, and then go for the love and religion stuff." He was, actually, a good man, but his theme song,

 "I love me, I love me,
I'm wild about myself . . ."

got monotonous after a while. It was a death chant; it made what might have been a fine man a man who was something far less attractive.

For most babies (thank heaven and good mothers!) there comes the day when each one begins to understand the sacrifices Mother and Dad are making for him, and when he looks at them and says, "I love you," and means it. This is the age when "My father can lick your father!" The child will fight to protect his younger brother. He is learning the first disciplines of life. He is becoming aware of others, and the niceness in others. He knows teenage love. He meets and loves the only girl in the world, and he'd *die* for her. All the world is lovely then.

But he'd better be careful. This is the dangerous age, in which a careless or misplaced love can be prelude to disaster. It may be infatuation rather than love that leads him to woo and marry the girl—only to discover that he shouldn't have married her at all. Remember the war brides who married the man in uniform after a ten-day acquaintance and then wrote him a "Dear John" letter before he was through fighting?

Or he may see the one he loves take off with a teenage rival, which leaves him a mooning, mourning, broken-hearted wreck of an old man

78

at seventeen. It may be the best thing that ever happened to him; twenty years later he may have difficulty recalling the name of that first girl.

Or he may find Miss Right in these teenage years—find the rapture and the ecstasy of a love that laughs at the passing years and grows stronger with time. It happens more often than we think. There is no lovelier love.

Yes, love is as tricky as skating on thin ice.

Or it can be another style of love that leads to other unexpected trouble. Love of what the teenager thinks is fun can put him in the local jail; love of what he thinks is freedom can make him a killer when he gets his driving license at seventeen; love of the "right" to live his own life and-the-devil-take-those-who-don't-like-it can make him a boor and a bore and a pest. Even that admirable love of country (of which we have too little now) can leave him dead and forgotten in some senseless Vietnam. Love can be dynamite when practiced heedlessly; it can inspire and it can kill.

Still, all this represents a progress in understanding the meaning of love from the days of infancy. There has been growth from mere self-love; the circle is widening. The good love that ruled in the family creeps out of doors and windows to *others*. It reaches the immigrant boy who lives down the street; it goes to the black boy who is fullback on the high school or college team. We hear of a Mahatma Gandhi or a Sir Winston or an Albert Schweitzer and we say, "There was a great man!" Love moves out.

And then one day we come to look into the face of Jesus Christ and we say, "There was the greatest of them all!" The greatest man, the greatest love, the *ultimate* love, love without bounds, the very love of God. Perfect love arrived on earth in the Nazarene who taught us that love must be all-inclusive, all-embracing, international, or it is not love at all. He taught us by his own example that *love is something you do*—you do it not for yourself but for your neighbor, whether he lives in Middletown or Mozambique.

Men ridiculed his idea that love means doing good (wishing good) for your enemies as well as your friends; men said he was "impractical," a fool, a dreamer, a subversive, a threat to those who loved war and profit and power; men murdered him in hatred and he accepted it in love, and prayed for them as he looked down on them from the cross.

We still say it; we still say his love is impractical "in our kind of world" (which is not as bad as the world he lived in). But is it an impractical, impossible love? What is practical about its opposite, in which we have for so long put our trust? What is practical about its opposite: hate? What is practical about our wars, which have resulted only in more wars? What is practical about our racial conflict? What is practical about the man who says, "I'll get mine," and ignores half his hungry world and then wonders why the hungry run out of patience, and revolt? The New Testament is right when it says that we who say we love God and hate our fellow men are a pack of liars.

We say his brand of love is impossible?

How do we know, until we've tried it?

We've met some who have tried it, and it seems to work.

A few months ago we sat with a group of friends splashing our feet in the pool of a million-dollar luxury hotel in South America. One of the party said to us, "I won't be with you tomorrow. I'm going to see a cousin of mine who is a priest on top of that mountain." The mountain was twenty miles away; our friend had quite a trip getting up there. He went part of the way in a Cadillac, transferred to a jeep and then to a horse, then a guide led him up a long flight of crude stone steps cut out of the mountainside—cut by the little priest who had come out there from the Bronx to help a people he had never seen.

In the village when he first came, there was the kind of poverty so appalling that it cut one's breath. Sewage ran in the open gutter of the only street; men and women in rags and filth, children with no clothes at all, lived in shacks made of battered tin signs and rotten wood. There was no school, no church—only the silent, brooding despair of a crushed and sullen people. The little priest took off his coat, recruited a few helpers and dug ditches for sewer pipes; he helped them tear down the shacks and build houses fit to live in, and at one end of the village he built a little schoolhouse, and in one corner of the schoolhouse he set up an altar at which he prayed. The children, until they got to know him, snickered at the funny, kneeling man, but one by one they started to sneak up behind him and kneel, and then a few brave adults drifted in, and in time the room wouldn't hold them and they asked for a church. *Asked* for it! The priest never suggested that they build a church nor that they even have a church—but because his example of love for them was so powerful, they *wanted* to come, *wanted* a church, *wanted* to pray!

My friend stood with the priest on a little balcony and looked down at the busy street. "Look at them," said the priest. "Aren't they a *beautiful* people?" The visitor hadn't noticed that before; he saw now that they *were* a beautiful people, walking with their heads up, their faces gleaming, their shoulders squared—they walked as though they were going somewhere. They walked as though they had been baptized with a new spirit. . . .

The cousin asked the priest, "How will it all end? Will it last, or . . . ?"

"It will last. I will die here, someday. Someone, some assassin will come up here and kill me. [A dictatorial government hated this man; he had put dangerous ideas of freedom and justice in the minds of these people, and that was bad.] But—so what? So what if they do kill me? I have done my work; these people now know the love of God, and they will never let it go."

He was already a fatally ill man; he had a disease called "terminal" which needed hospital treatment. But he said he couldn't get that treatment unless he gave up and went home, and he couldn't go home because if he did his superiors in his order would not let him return to the village on the mountain—they didn't like his unorthodox ways, and because he had broken every rule in the book, they would never let him go back. No, he didn't want to go home; he wanted to die here, among his people—his beautiful people.

That's love. It is about as close as a human being can come to perfect love.

We don't have to go to South America to find it; it is practiced every day right under our noses, right here at home. Some years ago, when Eddie Cantor suffered a coronary attack and was rushed to a hospital, Jimmy Durante went to see him, but the "No Visitors" sign was up on Eddie's door, so Jimmy dragged a chair down the corridor and propped it up against the wall just outside the door, and every day, until Eddie came home, Jimmy came and just sat there, for half an hour. He'd say to a nurse entering the room, "Just tell Eddie I'm out here, prayin'."

That's love—good, true, solid love.

My next-door neighbor died last week; like Eddie Cantor, it was a heart attack, but my neighbor died. We called the ambulance, the first aid corps, and traffic stopped in our streets as it raced to his door. For three quarters of an hour that ambulance crew worked feverishly to save him, but it didn't help. As they packed up their life-saving machinery, they were apologetic because they hadn't been able to work a miracle and save a man's life. They did all they could. They weren't paid a dime for that night's work, and they didn't want any pay. They were a beautiful people, that ambulance crew. . . .

The missionary priest, Jimmy Durante sitting by the door, the ambulance crew of total strangers I may never see again—these are the people who know what love *is*. *They know that love is something you do.*

You can have your men who have slugged their way to great wealth; they have no power in the Kingdom of God and we will do well to remember that Jesus paid very little attention to them. You can have your political princes playing the grim game of armaments with each other, selling nuclear reactors to Egypt one day and to Israel the next; if that is the best we can do, after nineteen hundred years of Jesus Christ, then, Father, forgive us, for we *know* what we are doing, and we are *not* doing it in love. I'll take the priest up there on the mountain. I'll take Jimmy out there in the hospital corridor. I'll ride with the beautiful people who ride the ambulance. . . . They know what love means, and they practice it.

Love! We can smile at the word as a description of adolescent sentimentality, we can debase and deprave it and make of it the filthy thing we call pornography, we can call it something for women and kids, but until we get a change of heart and begin to "do" love toward those we now shun and despise, we will never get to first base in our attempt to solve our racial problem or our armaments problem or any other problem foreign or domestic. We've tried just about everything *but* love, and here we are, a world of four billion people frightened out of our wits, the prisoners of fear cringing at the thought of a bomb that *can* drop on us and wipe out every last one of us in one cloud of nuclear dust.

Faith, hope, love—and the greatest of these is love. There is in the end no other way—no way, no way at all.

Frank S. Mead

82

A dream

THE CASTLE-BUILDER

A gentle boy, with soft and silken locks,
    A dreamy boy, with brown and tender eyes,
A castle-builder, with his wooden blocks,
    And towers that touch imaginary skies.
A fearless rider on his father's knee,
    An eager listener unto stories told
At the Round Table of the nursery,
    Of heroes and adventures manifold.
There will be other towers for thee to build;
    There will be other steeds for thee to ride;
There will be other legends, and all filled
    With greater marvels and more glorified.
Build on, and make thy castles high and fair,
    Rising and reaching upward to the skies;
Listen to voices in the upper air,
    Nor lose thy simple faith in mysteries.
Henry Wadsworth Longfellow

Romance

And what is a kiss, when all is done?
A promise given under seal—a vow,
A signature acknowledged—a rosy dot
Over the i of Loving—a secret whispered
To listening lips apart—a moment made
Immortal, with a rush of wings unseen—
A sacrament of blossoms, a new song
Sung by two hearts to an old simple tune—
The ring of one horizon around two souls
Together, all alone!

Edmond Rostand

What we behold is censured by our eyes.
Where both deliberate, the love is slight:
Who ever loved that loved not at first sight?
Christopher Marlowe

ANNABEL LEE

It was many and many a year ago,
    In a kingdom by the sea,
That a maiden there lived whom you may know
    By the name of Annabel Lee;—
And this maiden she lived with no other thought
    Than to love and be loved by me.

She was a child and I was a child,
    In this kingdom by the sea,
But we loved with a love that was more than love—
    I and my Annabel Lee—
With a love that the winged seraphs of Heaven
    Coveted her and me.

And this was the reason that, long ago,
    In this kingdom by the sea,
A wind blew out of a cloud, by night
    Chilling my Annabel Lee;
So that her highborn kinsmen came
    And bore her away from me,
To shut her up in a sepulchre
    In this kingdom by the sea.

The angels, not half so happy in Heaven,
    Went envying her and me:
Yes! that was the reason (as all men know,
    In this kingdom by the sea)
That the wind came out of the cloud, chilling
    And killing my Annabel Lee.

But our love it was stronger by far than the love
Of those who were older than we—
    Of many far wiser than we—
And neither the angels in Heaven above
    Nor the demons down under the sea,
Can ever dissever my soul from the soul
    Of the beautiful Annabel Lee:—

For the moon never beams without bringing me dreams
    Of the beautiful Annabel Lee;
And the stars never rise but I see the bright eyes
    Of the beautiful Annabel Lee;

And so, all the night-tide, I lie down by the side
Of my darling, my darling, my life and my bride,
   In her sepulchre there by the sea—
   In her tomb by the sounding sea.

Edgar Allan Poe

From ROMEO AND JULIET

He jests at scars, that never felt a wound.
But, soft! what light through yonder window breaks!
It is the east, and Juliet is the sun!
Arise, fair sun, and kill the envious moon,
Who is already sick and pale with grief,
That thou her maid art far more fair than she:
But be not her maid, since she is envious;
Her vestal livery is but sick and green,
And none but fools do wear it; cast it off.
It is my lady; O! it is my love:
O! that she knew she were.
She speaks, yet she says nothing: what of that?
Her eye discourses; I will answer it.
I am too bold, 'tis not to me she speaks:
Two of the fairest stars in all the heaven,
Having some business, do entreat her eyes
To twinkle in their spheres till they return.
What if her eyes were there, they in her head?
The brightness of her cheek would shame those stars
As daylight doth a lamp; her eyes in heaven
Would through the airy region stream so bright
That birds would sing and think it were not night.
See! how she leans her cheek upon her hand:
O! that I were a glove upon that hand,
That I might touch that cheek.

William Shakespeare

THE FIRST DAY

I wish I could remember the first day,
First hour, first moment of your meeting me,
If bright or dim the season, it might be
Summer or Winter for aught I can say;
So unrecorded did it slip away,
So blind was I to see and to foresee,
So dull to mark the budding of my tree
That would not blossom yet for many a May.
If only I could recollect it, such
A day of days! I let it come and go
As traceless as a thaw of bygone snow;
It seemed to mean so little, meant so much;
If only now I could recall that touch,
First touch of hand in hand—Did one but know!
Christina Rossetti

YOU SAY I LOVE NOT

You say I love not, 'cause I do not play
Still with your curls and kiss the time away.
You blame me, too, because I can't devise
Some sport to please those babies in your eyes:
By love's religion, I must here confess it,
The most I love when I the least express it.
Small griefs find tongues; full casks are ever found
To give, if any, yet but little sound.
Deep waters noiseless are; and this we know,
That chiding streams betray small depths below.
So when Love speechless is she doth express
A depth in love, and that depth bottomless.
Now since my love in tongueless, know me such,
Who speak but little 'cause I love so much.
Robert Herrick

Know you the land where the lemon-trees bloom?
In the dark foliage the gold oranges glow,
A soft wind hovers from the sky,
The myrtle is still and the laurel stands tall—
Do you know it well?
There, there, I would go, O my beloved, with thee!
Johann Wolfgang von Goethe

Absence lessens half-hearted passions, and increases great ones, as the wind puts out the candle and yet stirs up the fire.
La Rochefoucauld

THE GOOD MORROW

I wonder, by my troth, what thou and I
Did, till we loved? Were we not weaned till then,
But sucked on country pleasures, childishly?
Or snorted we in the seven sleepers' den?
'Twas so; but this, all pleasures fancies be.
If ever any beauty I did see,
Which I desired, and got, 'twas but a dream of thee.

And now good morrow to our waking souls,
Which watch not one another out of fear;
For love all love of other sights controls,
And makes one little room an everywhere.
Let sea-discoverers to new worlds have gone,
Let maps to other, worlds on worlds have shown;
Let us possess one world, each hath one, and is one.

My face in thine eye, thine in mine appears,
And true plain hearts do in the faces rest;
Where can we find two better hemispheres
Without sharp north, without declining west?
Whatever dies was not mixed equally;
If our two loves be one, or thou and I
Love so alike that none do slacken, none can die.
John Donne

THE DIFFERENCE BETWEEN ROMANCE AND LOVE *

It is easy to mistake romance for love. Yet there are many differences:

Romance is fleeting. . . . Love is long.

Romance is dancing in the moonlight. Gazing deep into desired eyes across a candlelit table . . . Love is saying: "You're tired, honey, I'll get up this time"—and stumbling through the darkness to warm a bottle or comfort a frightened child.

Romance is suspense, anticipation, surprise. . . . Love is dependability.

Romance is tingling excitement. . . . Love is tenderness, constancy, being cherished.

Romance is generally based on opposition, risks and denials. (Who'd ever have heard of Romeo and Juliet if their parents hadn't objected?) . . . Love is more often based on a similar background where parents and friends approve, even encourage: "Good. You were made for each other."

Romance is an eager striving always to appear attractive to each other. . . . Love is two people who find beauty in each other no matter how they look.

Romance is flattering attentions. . . . Love is genuine thoughtfulness.

Love is heightened and sweetened by romance, but it can survive without it. . . . Romance feeds only on itself and thus is self-consuming.

Romance is delicious. . . . Love nourishes.

Romance is seeking perfection. . . . Love is forgiving faults.

Romance is flying. . . . Love is safe landing.

Romance is the anguish of waiting for the phone to ring to bring you a voice that will utter endearments. . . . Love is the anguish of waiting for a call that will assure you someone else is happy and safe.

Romance can't last. . . . Love can't help it.

Marjorie Holmes

Excitement

My letters! all dead paper, mute and white!
And yet they seem alive and quivering
Against my tremulous hands which loose the string
And let them drop down on my knee to-night.
This said, —he wished to have me in his sight
Once, as a friend: this fixed a day in spring
To come and touch my hand . . . a simple thing,
Yet I wept for it!—this, . . . the paper's light . . .
Said, Dear, I love thee; and I sank and quailed
As if God's future thundered on my past.
This said, I am thine—and so its ink has paled
With lying at my heart that beat too fast.
And this . . . O Love, thy words have ill availed,
If, what this said, I dared repeat at last!
Elizabeth Barrett Browning

The man who has seen the rising moon break out of the clouds at midnight has been present like an archangel at the creation of light and of the world.

Ralph Waldo Emerson

LOCHINVAR

Oh, young Lochinvar is come out of the West,—
Through all the wide Border his steed was the best,
And save his good broadsword he weapons had none,—
He rode all unarm'd and he rode all alone.
So faithful in love, and so dauntless in war,
There never was knight like the young Lochinvar.

He stay'd not for brake, and he stopp'd not for stone,
He swam the Eske river where ford there was none,
But ere he alighted at Netherby gate,
The bride had consented, the gallant came late;
For a laggard in love and a dastard in war
Was to wed the fair Ellen of brave Lochinvar.

So boldly he enter'd the Netherby hall,
'Mong bridesmen and kinsmen and brothers and all.
Then spoke the bride's father, his hand on his sword
(For the poor craven bridegroom said never a word),
"Oh, come ye in peace here or come ye in war,
Or to dance at our bridal, young Lord Lochinvar?"

"I long woo'd your daughter, —my suit you denied;
Love swells like the Solway, but ebbs like its tide;
And now am I come, with this lost love of mine
To lead but one measure, drink one cup of wine.
There are maidens in Scotland more lovely, by far,
That would gladly be bride to the young Lochinvar."

The bride kissed the goblet, the knight took it up,
He quaff'd off the wine and he threw down the cup.
She look'd down to blush, and she look'd up to sigh,
With a smile on her lips and a tear in her eye.
He took her soft hand ere her mother could bar:
"Now tread we a measure," said young Lochinvar.

So stately his form, and so lovely her face,
That never a hall such a galliard did grace,
While her mother did fret, and her father did fume,
And the bridegroom stood dangling his bonnet and plume,
And the bridesmaidens whisper'd, " 'Twere better by far
To have match'd our fair cousin with young Lochinvar."

One touch to her hand, and one word in her ear,
When they reach'd the hall-door, and the charger stood near;
So light to the croupe the fair lady he swung,
So light to the saddle before her he sprung!
"She is won! we are gone, over bank, bush, and scour;
They'll have fleet steeds that follow," quoth young Lochinvar.

There was mounting 'mong Graemes of the Netherby clan;
Forsters, Fenwicks, and Musgraves, they rode and they ran;
There was racing and chasing on Connobie Lee,
But the lost bride of Netherby ne'er did they see.
So daring in love, and so dauntless in war,
Have ye e'er heard of gallant like young Lochinvar?

Sir Walter Scott

Tranquillity

OUT IN THE FIELDS WITH GOD

The little cares that fretted me,
    I lost them yesterday,
Among the fields above the sea,
    Among the winds at play,
Among the lowing of the herds,
    The rustling of the trees,
Among the singing of the birds,
    The humming of the bees.

The foolish fears of what might pass
    I cast them all away
Among the clover-scented grass
    Among the new-mown hay,
Among the rustling of the corn
    Where drowsy poppies nod,
Where ill thoughts die and good are born—
    Out in the fields with God!

Author unknown

What secret trouble stirs thy heart?
Why all this fret and flurry?
Dost thou not know that what is best
In this too restless world is rest
From over-work and hurry?
Henry Wadsworth Longfellow

From THE PRACTICE OF THE PRESENCE OF GOD

There is not in the world a kind of life more sweet and delightful than that of a continual conversation with God. Those only can comprehend it who practice and experience it; yet I do not advise you to do it from that motive. It is not pleasure which we ought to seek in this exercise; but let us do it from a principle of love, and because God would have us.

Were I a preacher, I should, above all other things, preach the practice of the presence of God; and were I a director, I should advise all the world to do it, so necessary do I think it, and so easy, too.

Ah! knew we but the want we have of the grace and assistance of God, we should never lose sight of Him—no, not for a moment. Believe me; make immediately a holy and firm resolution nevermore wilfully to forget Him, and to spend the rest of your days in His sacred presence, deprived, for the love of Him, if He thinks fit, of all consolations.

Set heartily about this work, and if you do it as you ought, be assured that you will find the effects of it.

Brother Lawrence

When we say, then, that pleasure is the end and aim of life, we do not mean the pleasures of the prodigal or the pleasures of sensuality. . . . By pleasure we mean the absence of pain in the body and of trouble in the soul.

Epicurus

96

When music spills from golden throat
  In wild bird reveille,
I push the drab world out in space
  And live in melody.
When color glows in countless ways
  Before my hungry eyes,
I am a gourmand at the feast
  Unmindful of how time flies,
For when this pageantry is spread
I quite forget my daily bread.
When cool waves run to greet the sands
  And whisper deep-sea lore,
I stand, at crimson close of day,
  Enchanted on the shore.
Each season wafts in new delights
  As beauty flames its way,
On rock, and earth, and sky, and sea,
  With respite for the day—
And oh, my dear, I humbly own
I cannot live by bread alone.
                    Christina Rossetti

Finish every day and be done with it. You have done what you could. Some blunders and absurdities no doubt crept in; forget them as soon as you can. Tomorrow is a new day; begin it well and serenely and with too high a spirit to be cumbered with your old nonsense. This day is all that is good and fair. It is too dear, with its hopes and invitations, to waste a moment on the yesterdays.
                    Ralph Waldo Emerson

The Lord is my shepherd, I shall not want;
    he makes me lie down in green pastures.
He leads me beside still waters;
    he restores my soul.
He leads me in paths of righteousness
    for his name's sake.

Even though I walk through the valley
    of the shadow of death,
    I fear no evil;
for thou art with me;
thy rod and thy staff, they comfort me.

Thou preparest a table before me
    in the presence of my enemies;
    thou anointest my head with oil,
my cup overflows.
Surely goodness and mercy shall follow me
    all the days of my life;
    and I shall dwell in the house of the Lord
    for ever.

Psalm 23, Revised Standard Version

Kind

The best portion of a good man's life,—
His little nameless unremembered acts
Of kindness and of love.

William Wordsworth

Be useful where thou livest, that they may
Both want and wish thy pleasing presence still.
  —Find out men's wants and will,
And meet them there. All worldly joys go less
To the one joy of doing kindnesses.

George Herbert

Do good to thy friend to keep him, to thy enemy to gain him.

Benjamin Franklin

WHEN LOVE IS KIND

When Love is kind,
Cheerful and free,
Love's sure to find
Welcome from me!

But when Love brings
Heartache or pang,
Tears and such things—
Love may go bang!

If Love can sigh
For one alone,
Well pleased am I
To be that one.

But should I see
Love giv'n to rove
To two or three,
Then—good-bye, Love!

Love must, in short,
Keep fond and true,
Through good report,
And evil too.

Else, here I swear,
Young Love may go,
For aught I care—
To Jericho.

Thomas Moore

THE NEW COLOSSUS

Not like the brazen giant of Greek fame,
With conquering limbs astride from land to land;
Here at our sea-washed, sunset gates shall stand
A mighty woman with a torch, whose flame
Is the imprisoned lightning, and her name
Mother of Exiles. From her beacon-hand
Glows world-wide welcome; her mild eyes command
The air-bridged harbor that twin cities frame.
"Keep, ancient lands, your storied pomp!" cries she
With silent lips. "Give me your tired, your poor,
Your huddled masses yearning to breathe free,
The wretched refuse of your teeming shore,
Send these, the homeless, tempest-tost to me,
I lift my lamp beside the golden door."

Emma Lazarus

COMFORT

Speak low to me, my Saviour, low and sweet
From out the hallelujahs, sweet and low,
Lest I should fear and fall, and miss Thee so,
Who art not missed by any that entreat.
Speak to me as to Mary at Thy feet!
And if no precious gums my hands bestow,
Let my tears drop like amber, while I go
In reach of Thy divinest voice complete
In humanest affection—thus, in sooth,
To lose the sense of losing. As a child,
Whose song-bird seeks the wood for evermore,
Is sung to in its stead by mother's mouth,
Till, sinking on her breast, love-reconciled,
He sleeps the faster that he wept before.

Elizabeth Barrett Browning

Faith

SOMEBODY LOVES YOU

SOMEBODY LOVES YOU more than you know,
SOMEBODY GOES WITH YOU wherever you go,
SOMEBODY REALLY and TRULY CARES
And LOVINGLY LISTENS TO ALL OF YOUR PRAYERS . . .

Don't doubt for a minute
   that this is not true,
For GOD loves HIS CHILDREN
   and takes care of them, too. . . .
And all of HIS TREASURES
   are yours to share
If you love HIM completely
   and show HIM you care. . . .
And if you "WALK IN HIS FOOTSTEPS"
   and have the FAITH to BELIEVE,
There's nothing you ask for
   that you will not receive!

Helen Steiner Rice

Every act of trust increases your capacity for God. Every time I trust Him I have more room for Him. He dwells within me in ever richer fullness, occupying room after room in my life. That is a glorious assurance, and one that is filled with infinite comfort.

John Henry Jowett

From THE ETERNAL GOODNESS

I see the wrong that round me lies,
  I feel the guilt within;
I hear, with groan and travail-cries,
  The world confess its sin.

Yet, in the maddening maze of things,
  And tossed by storm and flood,
To one fixed trust my spirit clings;
  I know that God is good!

I long for household voices gone,
  For vanished smiles I long,
But God hath led my dear ones on,
  And He can do no wrong.

I know not what the future hath
  Of marvel or surprise,
Assured alone that life and death
  His mercy underlies.
      John Greenleaf Whittier

SIR GALAHAD

My good blade carves the casques of men,
  My tough lance thrusteth sure,
My strength is as the strength of ten,
  Because my heart is pure.
The shattering trumpet shrilleth high,
  The hard brands shiver on the steel,
The splinter'd spear-shafts crack and fly,
  The horse and rider reel:
They reel, they roll in clanging lists,
  And when the tide of combat stands,
Perfume and flowers fall in showers,
  That lightly rain from ladies' hands.

How sweet are looks that ladies bend
  On whom their favours fall!
For them I battle till the end,
  To save from shame and thrall:
But all my heart is drawn above,
  My knees are bow'd in crypt and shrine:
I never felt the kiss of love,
  Nor maiden's hand in mine.
More bounteous aspects on me beam,
  Me mightier transports move and thrill;
So keep I fair thro' faith and prayer
  A virgin heart in work and will.

When down the stormy crescent goes,
  A light before me swims,
Between dark stems the forest glows,
  I hear a noise of hymns:
Then by some secret shrine I ride;
  I hear a voice, but none are there;
The stalls are void, the doors are wide,
  The tapers burning fair.
Fair gleams the snowy altar-cloth,
  The silver vessels sparkle clean,
The shrill bell rings, the censer swings,
  And solemn chaunts resound between.

Sometimes on lonely mountain-meres
  I find a magic bark;

I leap on board: no helmsman steers:
   I float till all is dark.
A gentle sound, an awful light!
   Three angels bear the holy Grail:
With folded feet, in stoles of white,
   On sleeping wings they sail.
Ah, blessed vision! blood of God!
   My spirit beats her mortal bars,
As down dark tides the glory slides,
   And star-like mingles with the stars.

When on my goodly charger borne
   Thro' dreaming towns I go,
The cock crows ere the Christmas morn,
   The streets are dumb with snow.
The tempest crackles on the leads,
   And, ringing, springs from brand and mail;
But o'er the dark a glory spreads,
   And gilds the driving hail.
I leave the plain, I climb the height;
   No branchy thicket shelter yields;
But blessed forms in whistling storms
   Fly o'er waste fens and windy fields.

A maiden knight—to me is given
   Such hope, I know not fear;
I yearn to breathe the airs of heaven
   That often meet me here.
I muse on joy that will not cease,
   Pure spaces clothed in living beams,
Pure lilies of eternal peace,
   Whose odours haunt my dreams;
And, stricken by an angel's hand,
   This mortal armour that I wear,
This weight and size, this heart and eyes,
   Are touch'd, are turn'd to finest air.

The clouds are broken in the sky,
   And thro' the mountain-walls
A rolling organ-harmony
   Swells up, and shakes and falls.
Then move the trees, the copses nod,

Wings flutter, voices hover clear:
"O just and faithful knight of God!
    Ride on! the prize is near."
So pass I hostel, hall, and grange;
    By bridge and ford, by park and pale,
All-arm'd I ride, whate'er betide,
    Until I find the holy Grail.

Alfred, Lord Tennyson

I will lift up mine eyes unto the hills,
    from whence cometh my help.
My help cometh from the Lord,
    which made heaven and earth.
He will not suffer thy foot to be moved:
    he that keepeth thee will not slumber.
Behold, he that keepeth Israel
    shall neither slumber nor sleep.
The Lord is thy keeper:
    the Lord is thy shade,
        upon thy right hand.
The sun shall not smite thee by day,
    nor the moon by night.
The Lord shall preserve thee from all evil:
    he shall preserve thy soul.
The Lord shall preserve thy going out
    and thy coming in
        from this time forth and even for evermore.

Psalm 121, King James Version

Beauty

SILENT NOON

Your hands lie open in the long fresh grass,—
The finger-points look through like rosy blooms:
Your eyes smile peace. The pasture gleams and glooms
'Neath billowing skies that scatter and amass.
All round our nest, far as the eye can pass,
Are golden kingcup-fields with silver edge
Where the cow-parsley skirts the hawthorn-hedge.
'Tis visible silence, still as the hour-glass.
Deep in the sun-searched growths the dragon-fly
Hangs like a blue thread loosened from the sky:—
So this winged hour is dropped to us from above.
Oh! clasp we to our hearts, for deathless dower,
This close-companioned inarticulate hour
When twofold silence was the song of love.

Dante Gabriel Rossetti

Beauty of whatever kind, in its supreme development, invariably excites the sensitive soul to tears.

Edgar Allan Poe

107

The essence of all beauty, I call love.
The attribute, the evidence, and end,
The consummation to the inward sense
Of beauty apprehended from without,
I still call love.

Elizabeth Barrett Browning

THE UNFADING BEAUTY

He that loves a rosy cheek,
  Or a coral lip admires,
Or from star-like eyes doth seek
  Fuel to maintain his fires:
As old Time makes this decay,
So his flames must waste away.

But a smooth and steadfast mind,
  Gentle thoughts and calm desires,
Hearts with equal love combined,
  Kindle never-dying fires.
Where these are not, I despise
Lovely cheeks or lips or eyes.

Thomas Carew

A loving heart carries with it, under every parallel of latitude, the warmth and light of the tropics. It plants its Eden in the wilderness and solitary place, and sows with flowers the gray desolation of rock and mosses.

John Greenleaf Whittier

I lived with visions for my company
Instead of men and women, years ago,
And found them gentle mates, nor thought to know
A sweeter music than they played to me.
But soon their trailing purple was not free
Of this world's dust, their lutes did silent grow,
And I myself grew faint and blind below
Their vanishing eyes. Then THOU didst come—to be,
Beloved, what they seemed. Their shining fronts,
Their songs, their splendours (better, yet the same,
As river-water hallowed into fonts)
Met in thee, and from out thee overcame
My soul with satisfaction of all wants—
Because God's gifts put man's best dreams to shame.
Elizabeth Barrett Browning

In all ranks of life the human heart yearns for the beautiful; and the beautiful things that God makes are his gift to all alike.
Harriet Beecher Stowe

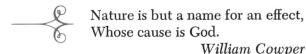 Nature is but a name for an effect,
Whose cause is God.
William Cowper

Apple orchards, the trees all covered with blossoms;
Wheat fields carpeted far and near in vital emerald green;
The eternal, exhaustless freshness of each early morning;
The yellow, golden, transparent haze of the warm afternoon sun;
The aspiring lilac bushes with profuse purple and white flowers.
Walt Whitman

She sweeps with many-colored brooms,
And leaves the shreds behind;
Oh, housewife in the evening West,
Come back, and dust the pond!

You dropped a purple ravelling in,
You dropped an amber thread;
And now you've littered all the East
With duds of emerald!

And still she plies her spotted brooms,
And still the aprons fly,
Till brooms fade softly into stars—
And then I come away.

Emily Dickinson

THE RAIN IS OVER AND GONE

The Cock is crowing,
The stream is flowing,
The small birds twitter,
The lake doth glitter,
The green field sleeps in the sun;
The oldest and youngest
Are at work with the strongest;
The cattle are grazing,
Their heads never raising;
There are forty feeding like one!

Like an army defeated
The snow hath retreated,
And now doth fare ill
On the top of the bare hill;
The ploughboy is whooping—anon—anon:
There's joy in the mountains;
There's life in the fountains;
Small clouds are sailing,
Blue sky prevailing;
The rain is over and gone!

William Wordsworth

110

I would rather hear a single shrub oak leaf at the end of a wintry glade rustle of its own accord at my approach, than receive a shipload of stars and garters from the strange kings and peoples of the earth.

Henry David Thoreau

Sensitivity

MY TRUE LOVE HATH MY HEART

My true love hath my heart, and I have his,
By just exchange one for the other given:
I hold his dear, and mine he cannot miss,
There never was a better bargain driven:
His heart in me keeps me and him in one,
My heart in his thoughts and senses guides:
He loves my heart, for once it was his own,
I cherish his because in me it bides:

His heart his wound received from my sight.
My heart was wounded with his wounded heart,
For as from me on him his heart did light,
So still methought in me his heart did smart,
Both equal hurt in this change sought our bliss:
My true love hath my heart, and I have his.

Sir Philip Sidney

Open to me thy heart of heart's deep core,
Or never say that I am dear to thee;
Call me not Friend, if thou keep close the door
That leads into thine inmost sympathy.

Oliver Wendell Holmes

The only true knowledge of our fellowman is that which enables us to feel with him . . . which gives us a fine ear for the heart pulses that are beating under the mere clothes of circumstances and opinion.

George Eliot

If I mayn't tell you what I feel, what is the use of a friend?

William Makepeace Thackeray

The language of friendship is not words, but meanings. It is an intelligence above language.

Henry David Thoreau

The world is so empty if one thinks only of mountains, rivers, and cities; but to know someone who thinks and feels with us, and who, though distant is close to us in spirit, this makes the earth for us an inhabited garden.

Johann Wolfgang von Goethe

Say over again, and yet once over again,
That thou dost love me. Though the word repeated
Should seem a "cuckoo-song," as thou dost treat it,
Remember, never to the hill or plain,
Valley and wood, without her cuckoo-strain
Comes the fresh Spring in all her green completed.
Beloved, I, amid the darkness greeted
By a doubtful spirit-voice, in that doubt's pain
Cry, "Speak once more—thou lovest!" Who can fear
Too many stars, though each in heaven shall roll,
Too many flowers, though each shall crown the year?
Say thou dost love me, love me, love me—toll
The silver iterance!—only minding, Dear,
To love me also in silence, with thy soul.

Elizabeth Barrett Browning

 There was a man with a tongue of wood
Who essayed to sing,
And in truth it was lamentable.
But there was one who heard
The clip-clapper of this tongue of wood
And knew what the man
Wished to sing,
And with that the singer was content.

Stephen Crane

Noble

The strong, calm man is always loved and revered.
James Allen

I think of the importance of friendship in the education of men. It will make a man honest; it will make him a hero; it will make him a saint. It is the state of the just dealing with the just, the magnanimous with the magnanimous, the sincere with the sincere, man with man.
Henry David Thoreau

No man or woman can really be strong, gentle, pure, and good without the world being better for it.

Phillips Brooks

Build me a son, O Lord, who will be strong enough to know when he is weak, and brave enough to face himself when he is afraid; one who will be proud and unbending in honest defeat, and humble and gentle in victory.

Build me a son whose wishbone will not be where his backbone should be; a son who will know Thee—and that to know himself is the foundation stone of knowledge.

Lead him, I pray, not in the path of ease and comfort, but under the stress and spur of difficulties and challenge. Here, let him learn to stand up in the storm; here, let him learn compassion for those who fail.

Build me a son whose heart will be clear, whose goal will be high; a son who will master himself before he seeks to master other men; one who will learn to laugh, yet never forget how to weep; one who will reach into the future, yet never forget the past.

And after all these things are his, add, I pray, enough of a sense of humor, so that he may always be serious, yet never take himself too seriously. Give him humility, so that he may always remember the simplicity of true greatness, the open mind of true wisdom, the meekness of true strength. Then I, his father, will dare to whisper: "I have not lived in vain."

General Douglas A. MacArthur

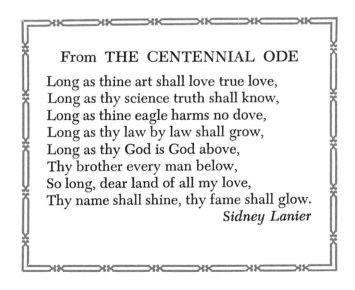

From THE CENTENNIAL ODE

Long as thine art shall love true love,
Long as thy science truth shall know,
Long as thine eagle harms no dove,
Long as thy law by law shall grow,
Long as thy God is God above,
Thy brother every man below,
So long, dear land of all my love,
Thy name shall shine, thy fame shall glow.
Sidney Lanier

The first time that the sun rose on thine oath
To love me, I looked forward to the moon
To slacken all those bonds which seemed too soon
And quickly tied to make a lasting troth.
Quick-loving hearts, I thought, may quickly loathe,
And, looking on myself, I seemed not one
For such man's love!—more like an out-of-tune
Worn viol, a good singer would be wroth
To spoil his song with, and which, snatched in haste,
Is laid down at the first ill-sounding note.
I did not wrong myself so, but I placed
A wrong on thee. For perfect strains may float
'Neath master-hands, from instruments defaced,—
And great souls, at one stroke, may do and doat.
Elizabeth Barrett Browning

From A TALE OF TWO CITIES

[EDITOR'S NOTE: It is 1775, and the French Revolution is reaching the height of frenzy. Hatred of the aristocratic landed classes, personal vengeance, retribution exacted for generations of wrongdoing against the underprivileged, have produced a nightmarish bloodbath in France.

Charles Darnay, brought up in England but a member of the aristocratic Évrémonde family in France, has been lured to Paris, arrested, and sentenced to die. In his cell on the eve of his execution he thinks of his wife and child, of his home in England, and of the life he soon must forfeit. Only hours before he is to be taken to the guillotine and public execution, he is surprised by a visit from Sidney Carton, a man he knew in England. Carton—a dissolute, hard-drinking failure of a man—bears an amazing physical resemblance to the doomed Darnay.]

In the black prison of the Conciergerie, the doomed of the day awaited their fate. They were in number as the weeks of the year. Fifty-two were to roll that afternoon on the life-tide of the city to the boundless everlasting sea. Before their cells were quit of them, new occupants were appointed; before their blood ran into the blood spilled yesterday, the blood that was to mingle with theirs to-morrow was already set apart.

Two score and twelve were told off. From the farmer-general of seventy, whose riches could not buy his life, to the seamstress of twenty, whose poverty and obscurity could not save her. Physical diseases, engendered in the vices and neglects of men, will seize on victims of all degrees; and the frightful moral disorder, born of unspeakable suffering, intolerable oppression, and heartless indifference, smote equally without distinction.

Charles Darnay, alone in a cell, had sustained himself with no flattering delusion since he came to it from the Tribunal. In every line of the narrative he had heard, he had heard his condemnation. He had fully comprehended that no personal influence could possibly save him, that he was virtually sentenced by the millions, and that units could avail him nothing.

Nevertheless, it was not easy, with the face of his beloved wife fresh before him, to compose his mind to what it must bear. His hold on life was strong, and it was very, very hard to loosen; by gradual efforts and degrees unclosed a little here, it clenched the tighter there; and when he brought his strength to bear on that hand and it yielded, this was closed again. There was a hurry, too, in all his thoughts, a turbulent and heated working of his heart, that contended against resignation. If, for a moment, he did feel resigned, then his wife and child, who had to live after him, seemed to protest and to make it a selfish thing.

But, all this was at first. Before long the consideration that there was no disgrace in the fate he must meet, and that numbers went the same road wrongfully, and trod it firmly every day, sprang up to stimulate him. Next followed the thought that much of the future peace of mind enjoyable by the dear ones depended on his quiet fortitude. So, by degrees he calmed into the better state, when he could raise his thoughts much higher, and draw comfort down.

Before it had set in dark on the night of his condemnation, he had travelled thus far on his last way. Being allowed to purchase the means of writing, and a light, he sat down to write until such time as the prison lamps should be extinguished.

He wrote a long letter to Lucie. . . . Next to her preservation of his own last grateful love and blessing, and her overcoming of her sorrow, to devote herself to their dear child, he adjured her, as they would meet in Heaven, to comfort her father.

To her father himself, he wrote in the same strain; but he told her father that he expressly confided his wife and child to his care. . . .

He had time to finish these letters before the lights were put out. When he lay down on his straw bed, he thought he had done with this world.

But, it beckoned him back in his sleep, and showed itself in shining forms. Free and happy, back in the old house in Soho (though it had nothing in it like the real house), unaccountably released and light of heart, he was with Lucie again, and she told him it was all a dream, and he had never gone away. A pause of forgetfulness, and then he had even suffered, and had come back to her, dead and at peace, and yet there was no difference in him. Another pause of oblivion, and he awoke in the sombre morning, unconscious where he was or what had happened, until it flashed upon his mind, "This is the day of my death!"

Thus, had he come through the hours, to the day when the fifty-two heads were to fall. And now, while he was composed, and hoped that he could meet the end with quiet heroism, a new action began in his waking thoughts, which was very difficult to master.

He had never seen the instrument that was to terminate his life. How high it was from the ground, how many steps it had, where he would be stood, how he would be touched, whether the touching hands would be dyed red, which way his face would be turned, whether he would be the first, or might be the last: these and many similar questions, in no wise directed by his will, obtruded themselves over and over again, countless times. Neither were they connected with fear: he was conscious of no fear. Rather, they originated in a strange besetting desire to know what to do when the time came; a desire gigantically disproportionate to the few split moments to which it referred; a wondering that was more like the wondering of some other spirit within him, than his own.

The hours went on as he walked to and fro, and the clocks struck the numbers he would never hear again. Nine gone for ever, ten gone for ever, eleven gone for ever, twelve coming on to pass away. After a hard contest with that eccentric action of thought which had last perplexed him, he had got the better of it. He walked up and down, softly repeating their names to himself. The worst of the strife was over. He could walk up and down, free from distracting fancies, praying for himself and for them.

Twelve gone for ever.

He had been apprised that the final hour was three, and he knew he would be summoned some time earlier, inasmuch as the

tumbrils jolted heavily and slowly through the streets. Therefore, he resolved to keep two before his mind, as the hour, and so to strengthen himself in the interval that he might be able, after that time, to strengthen others.

Walking regularly to and fro with his arms folded on his breast, a very different man from the prisoner who had walked to and fro at La Force, he heard one struck away from him, without surprise. The hour had measured like most other hours. Devoutly thankful to Heaven for his recovered self-possession, he thought, "There is but another now," and turned to walk again.

Footsteps in the stone passage outside the door. He stopped.

The key was put in the lock, and turned. Before the door was opened, or as it opened, a man said in a low voice, in English: "He has never seen me here; I have kept out of his way. Go you in alone; I wait near. Lose no time!"

The door was quickly opened and closed, and there stood before him face to face, quiet, intent upon him, with the light of a smile on his features, and a cautionary finger on his lip, Sydney Carton.

There was something so bright and remarkable in his look, that, for the first moment, the prisoner misdoubted him to be an apparition of his own imagining. But, he spoke, and it was his voice; he took the prisoner's hand, and it was his real grasp.

"Of all the people upon earth, you least expected to see me?" he said.

"I could not believe it to be you. I can scarcely believe it now. You are not"—the apprehension came suddenly into his mind—"a prisoner?"

"No. I am accidentally possessed of a power over one of the keepers here, and in virtue of it I stand before you. I come from her—your wife, dear Darnay."

The prisoner wrung his hand.

"I bring you a request from her."

"What is it?"

"A most earnest, pressing, and emphatic entreaty, addressed to you in the most pathetic tones of the voice so dear to you, that you well remember."

The prisoner turned his face partly aside.

"You have no time to ask me why I bring it, or what it means; I have no time to tell you. You must comply with it—take off those boots you wear, and draw on these of mine."

There was a chair against the wall of the cell, behind the prisoner. Carton, pressing forward, had already, with the speed of lightning, got him down into it, and stood over him, barefoot.

"Draw on those boots of mine. Put your hands to them: put your will to them. Quick!"

"Carton, there is no escaping from this place; it never can be done. You will only die with me. It is madness."

"It would be madness if I asked you to escape: but do I? When I ask you to pass out at that door, tell me it is madness and remain here. Change that cravat for this of mine, that coat for this of mine. While you do it, let me take this ribbon from your hair, and shake out your hair like this of mine!"

With wonderful quickness, and with a strength both of will and action, that appeared quite supernatural, he forced all these changes upon him. The prisoner was like a young child in his hands.

"Carton! Dear Carton! It is madness. It cannot be accomplished, it never can be done, it has been attempted, and has always failed. I implore you not to add your death to the bitterness of mine."

"Do I ask you, my dear Darnay, to pass the door? When I ask that, refuse. There are pen and ink and paper on this table. Is your hand steady enough to write?"

"It was when you came in."

"Steady it again, and write what I shall dictate. Quick, friend, quick!"

Pressing his hand to his bewildered head, Darnay sat down at the table. Carton, with his right hand in his breast, stood close beside him.

"Write exactly as I speak."

"To whom do I address it?"

"To no one." Carton still had his hand in his breast.

"Do I date it?"

"No."

The prisoner looked up at each question. Carton, standing over him with his hand in his breast, looked down.

" 'If you remember,' " said Carton, dictating, " 'the words that passed between us, long ago, you will readily comprehend this when you see it. You do remember them, I know. It is not in your nature to forget them.' "

He was drawing his hand from his breast; the prisoner, chancing to look up in his hurried wonder as he wrote, the hand stopped, closing upon something.

"Have you written 'forget them'?" Carton asked.

"I have. Is that a weapon in your hand?"

"No; I am not armed."

"What is it in your hand?"

"You shall know directly. Write on; there are but a few words more." He dictated again. " 'I am thankful that the time has come, when I can prove them. That I do so is no subject for regret or grief.' " As he said these words with his eyes fixed on the writer, his hand slowly and softly moved down close to the writer's face.

The pen dropped from Darnay's fingers on the table, and he looked about him vacantly.

"What vapour is that?" he asked.

"Vapour?"

"Something that crossed me?"

"I am conscious of nothing; there can be nothing here. Take up the pen and finish. Hurry, hurry!"

As if his memory were impaired, or his faculties disordered, the prisoner made an effort to rally his attention. As he looked at Carton with clouded eyes and with an altered manner of breathing, Carton—his hand again in his breast—looked steadily at him.

"Hurry, hurry!"

The prisoner bent over the paper once more.

" 'If it had been otherwise' "—Carton's hand was again watchfully and softly stealing down—" 'I never should have used the longer op-

124

portunity. If it had been otherwise'"—the hand was at the prisoner's face—"'I should but have had so much the more to answer for. If it had been otherwise—'" Carton looked at the pen and saw it was trailing off into unintelligible signs.

Carton's hand moved back to his breast no more. The prisoner sprang up with a reproachful look, but Carton's hand was close and firm at his nostrils, and Carton's left arm caught him round the waist. For a few seconds he faintly struggled with the man who had come to lay down his life for him; but, within a minute or so, he was stretched insensible on the ground.

Quickly, but with hands as true to the purpose as his heart was, Carton dressed himself in the clothes the prisoner had laid aside, combed back his hair, and tied it with the ribbon the prisoner had worn. Then, he softly called, "Enter there! Come in!" and the spy presented himself.

"You see?" said Carton, looking up, as he kneeled on one knee beside the insensible figure, putting the paper in the breast: "is your hazard very great?"

"Mr. Carton," the spy answered, with a timid snap of his fingers, "my hazard is not that, in the thick of business here, if you are true to the whole of your bargain."

"Don't fear me. I will be true to the death."

"You must be, Mr. Carton, if the tale of fifty-two is to be right. Being made right by you in that dress, I shall have no fear."

"Have no fear! I shall soon be out of the way of harming you, and the rest will soon be far from here, please God! Now, get assistance and take me to the coach."

"You?" said the spy nervously.

"Him, man, with whom I have exchanged. You go out at the gate by which you brought me in?"

"Of course."

"I was weak and faint when you brought me in, and I am fainter now you take me out. The parting interview has overpowered me. Such a thing has happened here, often, and too often. Your life is in your own hands. Quick! Call assistance!"

"You swear not to betray me?" said the trembling spy, as he paused for a last moment.

"Man, man!" returned Carton, stamping his foot; "have I sworn by no solemn vow already, to go through with this, that you waste the precious moments now? Take him yourself to the courtyard you know of, place him yourself in the carriage, show him yourself to

Mr. Lorry, tell him yourself to give him no restorative but air, and to remember my words of last night, and his promise of last night, and drive away!"

The spy withdrew, and Carton seated himself at the table, resting his forehead on his hands. The spy returned immediately, with two men.

"How, then?" said one of them, contemplating the fallen figure. "So afflicted to find that his friend has drawn a prize in the lottery of Sainte Guillotine?"

"A good patriot," said the other, "could hardly have been more afflicted if the aristocrat had drawn a blank."

They raised the unconscious figure, placed it on a litter they had brought to the door, and bent to carry it away.

"The time is short, Évrémonde," said the spy, in a warning voice.

"I know it well," answered Carton. "Be careful of my friend, I entreat you, and leave me."

"Come then, my children," said Barsad. "Lift him, and come away!"

The door closed, and Carton was left alone. Straining his powers of listening to the utmost, he listened for any sound that might denote suspicion or alarm. There was none. Keys turned, doors clashed, footsteps passed along distant passages: no cry was raised or hurry made, that seemed unusual. Breathing more freely in a little while, he sat down at the table, and listened again until the clock struck two.

Sounds that he was not afraid of, for he divined their meaning, then began to be audible. Several doors were opened in succession, and finally his own. A gaoler, with a list in his hand, looked in, merely saying, "Follow me, Évrémonde!" and he followed into a large dark room, at a distance. It was a dark winter day, and what with the shadows within, and what with the shadows without, he could but dimly discern the others who were brought there to have their arms bound. Some were standing; some seated. Some were lamenting, and in restless motion; but, these were few. The great majority were silent and still, looking fixedly at the ground.

As he stood by the wall in a dim corner, while some of the fifty-

two were brought in after him, one man stopped in passing, to embrace him, as having a knowledge of him. It thrilled him with a great dread of discovery; but the man went on. A very few moments after that, a young woman, with a slight girlish form, a sweet spare face in which there was no vestige of colour, and large widely opened patient eyes, rose from the seat where he had observed her, sitting, and came to speak to him.

"Citizen Évrémonde," she said, touching him with her cold hand, "I am a poor little seamstress, who was with you in La Force."

He murmured for answer: "True. I forget what you were accused of?"

"Plots. Though the just Heaven knows I am innocent of any. Is it likely? Who would think of plotting with a poor little weak creature like me?"

The forlorn smile with which she said it so touched him, that tears started from his eyes.

"I am not afraid to die, Citizen Évrémonde, but I have done nothing. I am not unwilling to die, if the Republic which is to do so much good for us poor, will profit by my death; but I do not know how that can be, Citizen Évrémonde. Such a poor weak little creature!"

As the last thing on earth that his heart was to warm and soften to, it warmed and softened to this pitiable girl.

"I heard you were released, Citizen Évrémonde. I hoped it was true?"

"It was. But, I was again taken and condemned."

"If I may ride with you, Citizen Évrémonde, will you let me hold your hand? I am not afraid, but I am little and weak, and it will give me more courage."

As the patient eyes were lifted to his face, he saw a sudden doubt in them, and then astonishment. He pressed the work-worn, hunger-worn young fingers, and touched his lips.

"Are you dying for him?" she whispered.

"And his wife and child. Hush! Yes."

"Oh, you will let me hold your brave hand, stranger?"

"Hush! Yes, my poor sister; to the last."

. . . Along the Paris streets, the death-carts rumble, hollow and harsh. Six tumbrils carry the day's wine to La Guillotine. All the devouring and insatiate monsters imagined since imagination could record itself, are fused in the one realisation, Guillotine. And yet there is not in France, with its rich variety of soil and climate, a blade, a leaf, a root, a sprig, a peppercorn, which will grow to maturity under conditions more certain than those that have produced this horror. Crush humanity out of shape once more, under similar hammers, and it will twist itself into the same tortured forms. Sow the same seed of rapacious license and oppression over again, and it will surely yield the same fruit according to its kind. . . .

As the sombre wheels of the six carts go round, they seem to plough up a long crooked furrow among the populace in the streets. Ridges of faces are thrown to this side and to that, and the ploughs go steadily onward. So used are the regular inhabitants of the houses to the spectacle, that in many windows there are no people, and in some the occupation of the hands is not so much as suspended, while the eyes survey the faces in the tumbrils. Here and there, the inmate has visitors to see the sight; then he points his finger, with something of the complacency of a curator or authorised exponent, to this cart and to this, and seems to tell who sat here yesterday, and who there the day before.

Of the riders in the tumbrils, some observe these things, and all things on their last roadside, with an impassive stare; others, with a lingering interest in the ways of life and men. Some, seated with drooping heads, are sunk in silent despair; again, there are some so heedful of their looks that they cast upon the multitude such glances as they have seen in theatres, and in pictures. Several close their eyes, and think, or try to get their straying thoughts together. Only one, and he a miserable creature, of a crazed aspect, is so shattered and made drunk by horror, that he sings, and tries to dance. Not one of the whole number appeals, by look or gesture, to the pity of the people.

There is a guard of sundry horsemen riding abreast of the tumbrils, and faces are often turned up to some of them, and they are asked some questions. It would seem to be always the same questions,

for, it is always followed by a press of people towards the third cart. The horsemen abreast of the cart frequently point out one man in it with their swords. The leading curiosity is to know which is he; he stands at the back of the tumbril with his head bent down, to converse with a mere girl who sits on the side of the cart, and holds his hand. He has no curiosity or care for the scene about him, and always speaks to the girl. Here and there in the long street of St. Honoré, cries are raised against him. If they move him at all, it is only to a quiet smile, as he shakes his hair a little more loosely about his face. He cannot easily touch his face, his arms being bound.

On the steps of a church, awaiting the coming-up of the tumbrils, stands the spy and prison-sheep. He looks into the first of them: not there. He looks into the second: not there. He already asks himself, "Has he sacrificed me?" when his face clears, as he looks into the third.

"Which is Évrémonde?" says a man behind him.

"That. At the back there."

"With his hand in the girl's?"

"Yes."

The man cries, "Down, Évrémonde! To the Guillotine all aristocrats; down, Évrémonde!"

"Hush, hush!" the spy entreats him, timidly.

"And why not, citizen?"

"He is going to pay the forfeit: it will be paid in five minutes more. Let him be at peace."

But the man continuing to exclaim, "Down, Évrémonde!" the face of Évrémonde is for a moment turned towards him. Évrémonde then sees the spy, and looks attentively at him, and goes his way.

The clocks are on the stroke of three, and the furrow ploughed among the populace is turning round, to come on into the place of execution, and end. The ridges thrown to this side and to that, now crumble in and close behind the last plough as it passes on, for all are following to the Guillotine. In front of it, seated in chairs, as in a garden of public diversion, are a number of women, busily knitting. On one of the foremost chairs stands the Vengeance, looking about for her friend.

"Thèrése!" she cries, in her shrill tones. "Who has seen her? Thèrése Defarge!"

"She never missed before," says a knitting-woman of the sister-hood.

"No, nor will she miss now," cries the Vengeance, petulantly. "Thèrése!"

"Louder," the woman recommends.

Ay! Louder, Vengeance, much louder, and still she will scarcely hear thee. Louder yet, Vengeance, with a little oath or so added, and yet it will hardly bring her. Send other women up and down to seek her, lingering somewhere; and yet, although the messengers have done dread deeds, it is questionable whether of their own will they will go far enough to find her!

"Bad Fortune!" cries The Vengeance, stamping her foot in the chair, "and here are the tumbrils! And Évrémonde will be dispatched in a wink, and she not here! See her knitting in my hand, and her empty chair ready for her. I cry with vexation and disappointment!"

As The Vengeance descends from her elevation to do it, the tumbrils begin to discharge their loads. The ministers of Sainte Guillotine are robed and ready. Crash! —A head is held up, and the knitting-women who scarcely lifted their eyes to look at it a moment ago when it could think and speak, count One.

The second tumbril empties and moves on; the third comes up. Crash! —And the knitting-women, never faltering or pausing in their work, count Two.

The supposed Évrémonde descends, and the seamstress is lifted out next after him. He has not relinquished her patient hand in getting out, but still holds it as he promised. He gently places her with her back to the crashing engine that constantly shirrs up and falls, and she looks into his face and thanks him.

"But for you, dear stranger, I should not be so composed, for I am naturally a poor little thing, faint of heart; nor should I have been able to raise my thought to Him who was put to death, that we might have hope and comfort here to-day. I think you were sent to me by Heaven."

"Or you to me," says Sydney Carton. "Keep your eyes upon me, dear child, and mind no other object."

"I mind nothing while I hold your hand. I shall mind nothing when I let it go, if they are rapid."

"They will be rapid. Fear not!"

The two stand in the fast-thinning throng of victims, but they speak as if they were alone. . . .

"Brave and generous friend, will you let me ask you one last question? I am very ignorant, and it troubles me—just a little."

"Tell me what it is."

"I have a cousin, an only relative and an orphan, like myself, whom I love very dearly. She is five years younger than I, and she lives in a farmer's house in the south country. Poverty parted us, and she knows nothing of my fate—for I cannot write—and if I could, how should I tell her! It is better as it is."

"Yes, yes; better as it is."

"What I have been thinking as we came along, and what I am

still thinking now, as I look into your kind strong face which gives me much support, is this: If the Republic really does good to the poor, and they come to be less hungry, and in all ways to suffer less, she may live a long time: she may even live to be old."

"What then, my gentle sister?"

"Do you think"—the uncomplaining eyes in which there is so much endurance, fill with tears, and the lips part a little more and tremble—"that it will seem long to me, while I wait for her in the better land where I trust both you and I will be mercifully sheltered?"

"It cannot be, my child; there is no time there, and no trouble there."

"You comfort me so much! I am so ignorant. Am I to kiss you now? Is the moment come?"

"Yes."

She kisses his lips; he kisses hers; they solemnly bless each other. The spare hand does not tremble as he releases it; nothing worse than a sweet, bright constancy is in the patient face. She goes next before him—is gone; the knitting-women count Twenty-two.

"I am the Resurrection and the Life, saith the Lord: he that believeth in me, though he were dead, yet shall he live: and whosoever liveth and believeth in me shall never die."

The murmuring of many voices, the upturning of many faces, the pressing on of many footsteps in the outskirts of the crowd, so that it swells forward in a mass, like one great heave of water, all flashes away. Twenty-three.

They said of him, about the city that night, that it was the peacefulest man's face ever beheld there. Many added that he looked sublime and prophetic.

One of the most remarkable sufferers by the same axe—a woman—had asked at the foot of the same scaffold, not long before, to be allowed to write down the thoughts that were inspiring her. If he had given an utterance to his, and they were prophetic, they would have been these:

"I see Barsad, and Cly, Defarge, The Vengeance, the Juryman, the Judge, long ranks of the new oppressors who have risen on the destruction of the old, perishing by this retributive instrument, before it shall cease out of its present use. I see a beautiful city and a brilliant people rising from this abyss, and, in their struggles to be truly free, in their triumphs and defeats through long years to come, I see the evil of this time and of the previous time of which this is the natural birth, gradually making expiation for itself and wearing out.

"I see the lives for which I lay down my life, peaceful, useful, prosperous and happy, in that England which I shall see no more. I see her with a child upon her bosom, who bears my name. I see her father, aged and bent, but otherwise restored, and faithful to all men in his healing office, and at peace. I see the good old man, so long their friend, in ten years' time enriching them with all he has, and passing tranquilly to his reward.

"I see that I hold a sanctuary in their hearts, and in the hearts of their descendants, generations hence. I see her, an old woman, weeping for me on the anniversary of this day. I see her and her husband, their course done, lying side by side in their last earthly bed, and I know that each was not more honoured and held sacred in the other's soul, than I was in the souls of both.

"I see that child who lay upon her bosom and who bore my name, a man winning his way up in that path of life which once was mine. I see him winning it so well, that my name is made illustrious there by the light of his. I see the blots I threw upon it faded away. I see him, foremost of the just judges and honoured men, bringing a boy of my

132

name, with a forehead that I know and golden hair, to this place—then fair to look upon, with not a trace of this day's disfigurement—and I hear him tell the child my story, with a tender and faltering voice.

"It is a far, far better thing that I do, than I have ever done; it is a far, far better rest that I go to than I have ever known."

Charles Dickens

Truth is a gem that is found at a great depth; whilst on the surface of this world, all things are weighed by the false scale of custom.

George Gordon, Lord Byron

A tear

When I have seen by Time's fell hand defaced
The rich proud cost of outworn buried age;
When sometime lofty towers I see down-razed
And brass eternal slave to mortal rage;
When I have seen the hungry ocean gain
Advantage of the kingdom of the shore,
And the firm soil win of the watery main,
Increasing store with loss and loss with store;
When I have seen such interchange of state,
Or state itself confounded to decay;
Ruin hath taught me thus to ruminate,
That Time will come and take my love away.
   This thought is as a death, which cannot choose
   But weep to have that which it fears to lose.
William Shakespeare

GRIEF

It is twilight. A thick wet snow is slowly twirling around the newly lighted street-lamps, and lying in soft thin layers on the roofs, the horses' backs, people's shoulders and hats. The cab-driver, Iona Potapov, is quite white, and looks like a phantom; he is bent double as far as a human body can bend double; he is seated on his box, and never makes a move. If a whole snowdrift fell on him, it seems as if he would not find it necessary to shake it off. His little horse is also quite white, and remains motionless; its immobility, its angularity, and its straight wooden-looking legs, even close by gave it the appearance of a ginger-bread horse worth a kopeck. It is, no doubt, plunged in deep thought. If you were snatched from the plough, from your usual grey surroundings, and were thrown into this slough full of monstrous lights, unceasing noise and hurrying people, you too would find it difficult not to think.

Iona and his little horse have not moved from their place for a long while. They left their yard before dinner, and, up to now, not a "fare." The evening mist is descending over the town, the white lights of the lamps are replacing brighter rays, and the hubbub of the street is getting louder. "Cabby, for Viborg way!" suddenly hears Iona. "Cabby!"

Iona jumps, and through his snow-covered eyelashes, sees an officer in a greatcoat, with his hood over his head.

"Viborg way!" the officer repeats. "Are you asleep, eh? Viborg way!"

With a nod of assent Iona picks up the reins, in consequence of which layers of snow slip off the horse's back and neck. The officer seats himself in the sleigh, the cab-driver smacks his lips to encourage his horse, stretches out his neck like a swan, sits up, and, more from habit than necessity, brandishes his whip. The little horse also stretches his neck, bends his wooden-looking legs, and makes a move undecidedly.

"What are you doing, were-wolf!" is the exclamation Iona hears, from the dark mass moving to and fro as soon as they started.

"Where the devil are you going? To the r-r-right!"

"You do not know how to drive. Keep to the right!" calls the officer angrily.

A coachman from a private carriage swears at him; a passerby, who has run across the road and rubbed his shoulder against the horse's nose, looks at him furiously as he sweeps the snow from his sleeve. Iona shifts about on his seat as if he were on needles, moves his elbows as if he were trying to keep his equilibrium, and gapes about like someone suffocating, and who does not understand why and wherefore he is there.

"What scoundrels they all are!" jokes the officer. "One would think they had all entered into an agreement to jostle you or fall under your horse."

Iona looks round at the officer, and moves his lips. He evidently wants to say something, but the only sound that issues is a snuffle.

"What?" asks the officer.

Iona twists his mouth into a smile, and with an effort says hoarsely:

"My son, barin, died this week."

"Hm! What did he die of?"

Iona turns with his whole body towards his fare, and says:

"And who knows! They say high fever. He was three days in hospital, and then died. . . . God's will be done."

"Turn round! The devil!" sounded from the darkness. "Have you popped off, old doggie, eh? Use your eyes!"

"Go on, go on," said the officer, "otherwise we shall not get there by to-morrow. Hurry a bit!"

The cab-driver again stretches his neck, sits up, and, with a bad grace, brandishes his whip. Several times again he turns to look at his fare, but the latter had closed his eyes, and apparently is not disposed to listen. Having deposited the officer in the Viborg, he stops by the tavern, doubles himself up on his seat, and again remains motionless, while the snow once more begins to cover him and his horse. An hour, and another. . . . Then, along the footpath, with a squeak of goloshes, and quarrelling, came three young men, two of them tall and lanky, the third one short and hump-backed.

"Cabby, to the Police Bridge!" in a cracked voice calls the humpback. "The three of us for two griveniks!"

Iona picks up his reins, and smacks his lips. Two griveniks is not a fair price, but he does not mind if it is a ruble or five kopecks— to him it is all the same now, so long as they are wayfarers. The young men, jostling each other and using bad language, approach the sleigh, and all three at once try to get on to the seat; then begins a discussion which two shall sit and who shall be the one to stand. After wrangling, abusing each other, and much petulance, it was at last decided that the hump-back should stand, as he was the smallest.

"Now then, hurry up!" says the hump-back in a twanging voice, as he takes his place, and breathes in Iona's neck. "Old furry. Here mate, what a cap you have got, there is not a worse one to be found in all Petersburg! . . ."

"Hi—hi, —hi—hi," giggles Iona. "Such a . . ."

"Now you, 'such a,' hurry up, are you going the whole way at this pace? Are you? . . . Do you want it in the neck?"

"My head feels like bursting," says one of the lanky ones. "Last night at the Donkmasovs', Vaska and I drank the whole of four bottles of cognac."

"I don't understand what you lie for," said the other lanky one angrily; "you lie like a brute."

"God strike me, it's the truth!"

"It's as much a truth as that a louse coughs!"

"Hi, hi," grins Iona, "what gay young gentlemen!"

"Pshaw, go to the devil!" indignantly says the hump-back.

"Are you going to get on or not, you old pest? Is that the way to drive? Use the whip a bit! Go on, devil, go on, give it him well!"

Iona feels at his back the little man wriggling, and the tremble in his voice. His listens to the insults hurled at him, sees the people, and little by little the feeling of loneliness leaves him. The hump-back goes on swearing until he gets mixed up in some elaborate six-foot oath, or chokes with coughing. The lankies begin to talk about a certain Nadejda Petrovna, Iona looks round at them several times; he waits for a temporary silence, then, turning round again, he murmurs:

"My son—died this week."

"We must all die," sighed the hump-back, wiping his lips after an attack of coughing. "Now, hurry up, hurry up! Gentlemen, I really cannot go any farther like this! When will he get us there?"

"Well, just you stimulate him a little in the neck!"

"You old pest, do you hear, I'll bone your neck for you! If one treated the like of you with ceremony one would have to go on foot! Do you hear, old serpent Gorinytch! Or do you not care a spit?"

Iona hears rather than feels the blows they deal him.

"Hi, hi," he laughs. "They are gay young gentlemen, God bless 'em!"

"Cabby, are you married?" asks a lanky one.

"I? Hi, hi, gay young gentlemen! Now I have only a wife: the moist ground . . . Hi, ho, ho . . . that is to say, the grave! My son has died, and I am alive . . . A wonderful thing, death mistook the door . . . instead of coming to me, it went to my son. . . ."

Iona turns round to tell them how his son died, but at the moment, the hump-back, giving a little sigh, announces, "Thank God, they have at last reached their destination," and Iona watches them disappear through the dark entrance. Once more he is alone, and again surrounded by silence. . . . His grief, which had abated for a short while, returns and rends his heart with greater force. With an anxious and a hurried look, he searches among the crowds passing on either side of the street to find if there is just one person who will listen to him. But the crowds hurry by without noticing him or his trouble. Yet it is such an immense, illimitable grief. Should his heart break and the grief pour out, it would flow over the whole earth it seems, and yet, not one sees it. It has managed to conceal itself in such an insignificant shell that no one can see it even by day and with a light.

Iona sees a hall-porter with some sacking, and decides to talk to him.

"Friend, what sort of time is it?" he asks.

"Past nine. What are you standing here for? Move on."

Iona moves on a few steps, doubles himself up, and abandons himself to his grief. He sees it is useless to turn to people for help. In less than five minutes he straightens himself, holds up his head as if he felt some sharp pain, and gives a tug at the reins; he can bear it no longer, "The stables," he thinks, and the little horse, as if he understood, starts off at a trot.

About an hour and a half later Iona is seated by a large dirty stove. Around the stove, on the floor, on the benches, people are snoring; the air is thick and suffocatingly hot. Iona looks at the sleepers, scratches himself, and regrets having returned so early.

"I have not even earned my fodder," he thinks. "That's what's my trouble. A man who knows his job, who has had enough to eat, and his horse too, can always sleep peacefully."

A young cab-driver in one of the corners half gets up, grunts sleepily, and stretches towards a bucket of water.

"Do you want a drink?" Iona asks him.

"Don't I want a drink!"

"That's so? Your good health! But listen, mate—you know, my son is dead. . . . Did you hear? This week, in hospital. . . . It's a long story."

Iona looks to see what effect his words have, but sees none—the young man has hidden his face, and is fast asleep again. The old man sighs, and scratches his head. Just as much as the young one wanted to drink, the old man wanted to talk. It will soon be a week since his son died, and he has not been able to speak about it properly

138

to anyone. One must tell it slowly and carefully; how his son fell ill, how he suffered, what he said before he died, how he died. One must describe every detail of the funeral, and the journey to the hospital to fetch the defunct's clothes. His daughter Anissia remained in the village—one must talk about her too. Was it nothing he had to tell? Surely the listener would gasp and sigh, and sympathise with him? It is better, too, to talk to women; although they are stupid, two words are enough to make them sob.

"I'll go and look at my horse," thinks Iona; "there's always time to sleep. No fear of that!"

He puts on his coat, and goes to the stables to his horse. He thinks of the corn, the hay, the weather. When he is alone, he dare not think of his son; he could speak about him to anyone, but to think of him, and picture him to himself, is unbearably painful.

"Are you tucking in?" Iona asks his horse, looking at his bright eyes; "go on, tuck in, though we've not earned our corn, we can eat hay. Yes! I am too old to drive—my son could have, not I. He was a first-rate cab-driver. If only he had lived!"

Iona is silent for a moment, then continues:

"That's how it is, my old horse. There's no more Kuzma Ionitch. He has left us to live, and he went off pop. Now let's say, you had a foal, you were that foal's mother, and suddenly, let's say, that foal went and left you to live after him. It would be sad, wouldn't it?"

The little horse munches, listens, and breathes over his master's hand. . . .

Iona's feelings are too much for him, and he tells the little horse the whole story.

Anton Chekhov

From SILAS MARNER

Godfrey's wife was walking with slow, uncertain steps through the snow-covered Raveloe lanes, carrying her child in her arms.

This journey on New Year's Eve was a premeditated act of vengeance which she had kept in her heart ever since Godfrey, in a fit of passion, had told her he would sooner die than acknowledge her as his wife. There would be a great party at the Red House on New Year's Eve, she knew: her husband would be smiling and smiled upon, hiding her existence in the darkest corner of his heart. But she would mar his pleasure: she would go in her dingy rags, with her faded face, once as handsome as the best, with her little child that had its father's hair and eyes, and disclose herself to the Squire as his eldest son's wife. It is seldom that the miserable can help regarding their misery as a wrong inflicted by those who are less miserable. Molly knew that the cause of her dingy rags was not her husband's neglect, but the demon Opium to whom she was enslaved, body and soul, except in the lingering mother's tenderness that refused to give him her hungry child. She knew this well; and yet, in the moments of wretched, unbenumbed consciousness, the sense of her want and degradation transformed itself continually into bitterness towards Godfrey. He was well off; and if she had her rights she would be well off too. The belief that he repented his marriage, and suffered from it, only aggravated her vindictiveness.

. . . She had set out at an early hour, but had lingered on the road, inclined by her indolence to believe that if she waited under a warm shed the snow would cease to fall. She had waited longer than she knew, and now that she found herself belated in the snow-hidden ruggedness of the long lanes, even the animation of a vindictive purpose could not keep her spirit from failing. It was seven o'clock, and by this time she was not very far from Raveloe, but she was not familiar enough with those monotonous lanes to know how near she was to her journey's end. She needed comfort, and she knew but one comforter— the familiar demon in her bosom; but she hesitated a moment, after drawing out the black remnant, before she raised it to her lips. In that moment the mother's love pleaded for painful consciousness rather than oblivion—pleaded to be left in aching weariness, rather than to have the encircling arms benumbed so that they could not feel the dear burden. In another moment Molly had flung something away, but it was not the black remnant—it was an empty phial. And she walked on again under the breaking cloud, from which there came now and then the light of a quickly veiled star, for a freezing wind had sprung up since the snowing had ceased. But she walked always more and more drowsily, and clutched more and more automatically the sleeping child at her bosom.

Slowly the demon was working his will, and cold and weariness were his helpers. Soon she felt nothing but a supreme immediate longing that curtained off all futurity—the longing to lie down and sleep. She had arrived at a spot where her footsteps were no longer checked by a hedgerow, and she had wandered vaguely, unable to distinguish any objects, notwithstanding the wide whiteness around her, and the growing starlight. She sank down against a straggling furze bush, an easy pillow enough; and the bed of snow, too, was soft. She did not feel that the bed was cold, and did not heed whether the child would wake and cry for her. But her arms had not yet relaxed their instinctive clutch; and the little one slumbered on as gently as if it had been rocked in a lacetrimmed cradle.

But the complete torpor came at last: the fingers lost their tension, the arms unbent; then the little head fell away from the bosom, and the blue eyes opened wide on the cold starlight. At first there was a little peevish cry of "Mammy," and an effort to regain the pillowing arm and bosom; but mammy's ear was deaf, and the pillow seemed to be slipping away backward. Suddenly, as the child rolled downward on its mother's knees, all wet with snow, its eyes were caught by a bright glancing light on the white ground, and, with the ready transition of infancy, it was immediately absorbed in watching the bright living thing running towards it, yet never arriving. That bright living thing must be caught; and in an instant the child had slipped on all fours, and held out one little hand to catch the gleam. But the gleam would not be caught in that way, and now the head was held up to see where the cunning gleam came from. It came from a very bright place; and the little one, rising on its legs, toddled through the snow, the old grimy shawl in which it was wrapped trailing behind it, and the queer little bonnet dangling at its back—toddled on to the open door of Silas Marner's cottage, and right up to the warm hearth, where there was a bright fire of logs and sticks, which had thoroughly warmed the old sack (Silas's greatcoat) spread out on the bricks to dry. The little one, accustomed to be left to itself for long hours without notice from its mother, squatted down on the sack, and spread its tiny hands towards the blaze, in perfect contentment, gurgling and making many inarticulate communications to the cheerful fire, like a new-hatched gosling beginning to find itself comfortable. But presently the warmth had a lulling effect, and the little golden head sank down on the old sack, and the blue eyes were veiled by their delicate, half-transparent lids.

But where was Silas Marner while this strange visitor had come to his hearth? He was in the cottage, but he did not see the child. During the last few weeks, since he had lost his money, he had contracted the habit of opening his door and looking out from time to time, as if he thought that his money might be somehow coming back to him, or that some trace, some news of it, might be mysteriously on the road, and be caught by the listening ear or the straining eye. It was chiefly at night, when he was not occupied in his loom, that he fell into the repetition of an act for which he could have assigned no definite purpose, and which can hardly be understood except by those who have undergone a bewildering separation from a supremely loved object. In the evening twilight, and later whenever the night was not dark, Silas looked out on that narrow prospect round the Stone Pits, listening and gazing, not with hope, but with mere yearning and unrest.

This morning he had been told by some of his neighbours that it was New Year's Eve, and that he must sit up and hear the old year rung out and the new rung in, because that was good luck, and might bring his money back again. This was only a friendly Raveloe way of jesting with the half-crazy oddities of a miser, but it had perhaps

helped to throw Silas into a more than usually excited state. Since the oncoming of twilight he had opened his door again and again, though only to shut it immediately at seeing all distance veiled by the falling snow. But the last time he opened it the snow had ceased, and the clouds were parting here and there. He stood and listened, and gazed for a long while—there was really something on the road coming towards him then, but he caught no sign of it; and the stillness and the wide trackless snow seemed to narrow his solitude, and touched his yearning with the chill of despair. He went in again, and put his right hand on the latch of the door to close it—but he did not close it: he was arrested, as he had been already since his loss, by the invisible wand of catalepsy, and stood like a graven image, with wide but sightless eyes, holding open his door, powerless to resist either the good or evil that might enter there.

When Marner's sensibility returned, he continued the action which had been arrested, and closed his door, unaware of the chasm in his consciousness, unaware of any intermediate change, except that the light had grown dim, and that he was chilled and faint. He thought he had been too long standing at the door and looking out. Turning towards the hearth, where the two logs had fallen apart, and sent forth only a red, uncertain glimmer, he seated himself on his fireside chair, and was stooping to push his logs together, when, to his blurred vision, it seemed as if there were gold on the floor in front of the hearth. Gold!—his own gold—brought back to him as mysteriously as it had been taken away! He felt his heart begin to beat violently, and for a few moments he was unable to stretch out his hand and grasp the restored treasure. The heap of gold seemed to glow and get larger beneath his agitated gaze. He leaned forward at last, and stretched forth his hand; but instead of the hard coin with the familiar resisting outline, his fingers encountered soft, warm curls. In utter amazement, Silas fell on his knees and bent his head low to examine the marvel: it was a sleeping child—a round, fair thing, with soft yellow rings all over its head. Could this be his little sister come back to him in a dream— his little sister whom he had carried about in his arms for a year before she died, when he was a small boy without shoes or stockings? That

was the first thought that darted across Silas's black wonderment. Was it a dream? He rose to his feet again, pushed his logs together, and throwing on some dried leaves and sticks, raised a flame; but the flame did not disperse the vision—it only lit up more distinctly the little round form of the child and its shabby clothing. It was very much like his little sister. Silas sank into his chair powerless, under the double presence of an inexplicable surprise and a hurrying influx of memories. How and when had the child come in without his knowledge? He had never been beyond the door. But along with that question, and almost thrusting it away, there was a vision of the old home and the old streets leading to Lantern Yard—and within that vision another, of the thoughts which had been present with him in those far-off scenes. The thoughts were strange to him now, like old friendships impossible to revive; and yet he had a dreamy feeling that this child was somehow a message come to him from that far-off life: it stirred fibres that had never been moved in Raveloe—old quiverings of tenderness—old impressions of awe at the presentiment of some Power presiding over his life; for his imagination had not yet extricated itself from the sense of mystery in the child's sudden presence, and had formed no conjectures of ordinary natural means by which the event could have been brought about.

But there was a cry on the hearth: the child had awaked, and Marner stooped to lift it on his knee. It clung round his neck, and burst louder and louder into that mingling of inarticulate cries with "Mammy" by which little children express the bewilderment of waking. Silas pressed it to him, and almost unconsciously uttered sounds of hushing tenderness, while he bethought himself that some of his porridge, which had got cool by the dying fire, would do to feed the child with if it were only warmed up a little.

He had plenty to do through the next hour. The porridge, sweetened with some dry brown sugar from an old store which he had refrained from using for himself, stopped the cries of the little one, and made her lift her blue eyes with a wide quiet gaze at Silas, as he put the spoon into her mouth. Presently she slipped from his knee and began to toddle about, but with a pretty stagger that made Silas jump up and follow her lest she should fall against anything that would hurt her. But she only fell in a sitting posture on the ground, and began to pull at her boots, looking up at him with a crying face as if the boots hurt her. He took her on his knee again, but it was some time before it occurred to Silas's dull bachelor mind that the wet boots were the grievance, pressing on her warm ankles. He got them off with difficulty, and

Baby was at once happily occupied with the primary mystery of her own toes, inviting Silas, with much chuckling, to consider the mystery too. But the wet boots had at last suggested to Silas that the child had been walking on the snow, and this roused him from his entire oblivion of any ordinary means by which it could have entered or been brought into his house. Under the prompting of this new idea, and without waiting to form conjectures, he raised the child in his arms, and went to the door. As soon as he had opened it, there was the cry of "Mammy" again, which Silas had not heard since the child's first hungry waking. Bending forward, he could just discern the marks made by the little feet on the virgin snow, and he followed their track to the furze bushes. "Mammy!" the little one cried again and again, stretching itself forward so as almost to escape from Silas's arms, before he himself was aware that there was something more than the bush before him—that there was a human body, with the head sunk low in the furze, and half-covered with the shaken snow.

. . . There was a pauper's burial that week in Raveloe, and up Kench Yard at Batherley it was known that the dark-haired woman with the fair child, who had lately come to lodge there, was gone away again. That was all the express note taken that Molly had disappeared from the eyes of men. But the unwept death which, to the general lot, seemed as trivial as the summer-shed leaf was charged with the force of destiny to certain human lives that we know of, shaping their joys and sorrows even to the end.

Silas Marner's determination to keep the "tramp's child" was matter of hardly less surprise and iterated talk in the village than the robbery of his money. That softening of feeling towards him which dated from his misfortune, that merging of suspicion and dislike in a rather contemptuous pity for him as lone and crazy, was now accompanied with a more active sympathy, especially amongst the women. Notable mothers, who knew what it was to keep children "whole and sweet"; lazy mothers, who knew what it was to be interrupted in folding their arms and scratching their elbows by the mischievous propensities of children just firm on their legs, were equally interested in conjecturing how a lone man would manage with a two-year-old child on his hands, and were equally ready with their suggestions: the notable chiefly telling him what he had better do, and the lazy ones being emphatic in telling him what he would never be able to do.

Among the notable mothers, Dolly Winthrop was the one whose neighbourly offices were the most acceptable to Marner, for they were rendered without any show of bustling instruction.

. . . "Eh, Master Marner," said Dolly, "there's no call to buy, no more nor a pair o' shoes; for I've got the little petticoats as Aaron wore five years ago, and it's ill spending the money on them baby clothes, for the child 'ull grow like grass i' May, bless it—that it will."

And the same day Dolly brought her bundle, and displayed to Marner, one by one, the tiny garments in their due order of succession, most of them patched and darned, but clean and neat as fresh-sprung herbs. This was the introduction to a great ceremony with soap and water, from which Baby came out in new beauty, and sat on Dolly's knee, handling her toes and chuckling and patting her palms together with an air of having made several discoveries about herself, which she communicated by alternate sounds of "gug-gug-gug," and "Mammy." The "Mammy" was not a cry of need or uneasiness; Baby had been used to utter it without expecting either tender sound or touch to follow.

"Anybody 'ud think the angils in heaven couldn't be prettier," said Dolly, rubbing the golden curls and kissing them. "And to think of its being covered wi' them dirty rags—and the poor mother—froze to death; but there's Them as took care of it, and brought it to your door, Master Marner. The door was open, and it walked in over the snow, like as if it had been a little starved robin. Didn't you say the door was open?"

"Yes," said Silas, meditatively. "Yes—the door was open. The money's gone I don't know where, and this is come from I don't know where."

He had not mentioned to anyone his unconsciousness of the child's entrance, shrinking from questions which might lead to the fact he himself suspected—namely, that he had been in one of his trances.

"Ah," said Dolly, with soothing gravity, "it's like the night and the morning, and the sleeping and the waking, and the rain and the harvest —one goes and the other comes, and we know nothing how nor where. We may strive and scrat and fend, but it's little we can do arter all—the big things come and go wi' no striving o' our'n—they do, that they do; and I think you're in the right on it to keep the little un, Master Marner, seeing as it's been sent to you, though there's folks as thinks different.

146

You'll happen be a bit moithered with it while it's so little; but I'll come, and welcome, and see to it for you: I've a bit o' time to spare most days, for when one gets up betimes i' the morning, the clock seems to stan' still tow'rt ten, afore it's time to go about the victual. So, as I say, I'll come and see to the child for you, and welcome."

"Thank you . . . kindly," said Silas, hesitating a little. "I'll be glad if you'll tell me things. But," he added, uneasily, leaning forward to look at Baby with some jealousy, as she was resting her head backward against Dolly's arm, and eyeing him contentedly from a distance, "but I want to do things for it myself, else it may get fond o' somebody else, and not fond o' me. I've been used to fending for myself in the house—I can learn, I can learn."

"Eh, to be sure," said Dolly gently. "I've seen men as are wonderful handy wi' children. The men are awk'ard and contrairy mostly, God help 'em—but when the drink's out of 'em, they aren't unsensible, though they're bad for leeching and bandaging—so fiery and unpatient. You see this goes first, next the skin," proceeded Dolly, taking up the little shirt, and putting it on.

"Yes," said Marner docilely, bringing his eyes very close, that they might be initiated in the mysteries; whereupon Baby seized his head with both her small arms, and put her lips against his face with purring noises.

"See there," said Dolly, with a woman's tender tact, "she's fondest o' you. She wants to go o' your lap, I'll be bound. Go, then: take her, Master Marner; you can put the things on, and then you can say as you've done for her from the first of her coming to you."

Marner took her on his lap, trembling with an emotion mysterious to himself, at something unknown dawning on his life. Thought and feeling were so confused he could only have said that the child was come instead of the gold—that the gold had turned into the child. He took the garments from Dolly, and put them on under her teaching; interrupted, of course, by Baby's gymnastics.

"There, then! why, you take to it quite easy, Master Marner," said Dolly; "but what shall you do when you're forced to sit in your loom? For she'll get busier and mischievouser every day—she will, bless her.

It's lucky as you've got that high hearth i'stead of a grate, for that keeps the fire more out of her reach; but if you've got anything as can be split or broke, or as is fit to cut her fingers off, she'll be at it—and it is but right you should know."

Silas meditated a little while in some perplexity. "I'll tie her to the leg o' the loom," he said at last, "tie her with a good long strip o' something."

"Well, mayhap that'll do, as it's a little gell, for they're easier persuaded to sit i' one place nor the lads. I know what the lads are; for I've had four—four I've had, God knows—and if you was to take and tie 'em up, they'd make a fighting and a crying as if you was ringing pigs. But I'll bring you my little chair, and some bits o' red rag and things for her to play wi'; an' she'll sit and chatter to 'em as if they was alive. Eh, if it wasn't a sin to the lads to wish 'em made different, bless 'em, I should ha' been glad for one of 'em to be a little gell; and to think as I could ha' taught her to scour, and mend, and the knitting, and everything. But I can teach 'em this little un, Master Marner, when she gets old enough."

"But she'll be my little un," said Marner rather hastily, "she'll be nobody else's."

"No, to be sure; you'll have a right to her if you're a father to her, and bring her up according. But," added Dolly, coming to a point which she had determined beforehand to touch upon, "you must bring her up like christened folk's children, and take her to church, and let her learn her catechise, as my little Aaron can say off—the 'I believe,' and everything, and 'hurt nobody by word or deed,'—as well as if he was the clerk. That's what you must do, Master Marner, if you'd do the right thing by the orphin child."

Marner's pale face flushed suddenly under a new anxiety. His mind was too busy trying to give some definite bearing to Dolly's words for him to think of answering her.

"And it's my belief," she went on, "as the poor little creature has never been christened, and it's nothing but right as the parson should be spoke to; and if you was noways unwilling, I'd talk to Mr. Macey about it this very day. For if the child ever went anyways wrong, and you hadn't done your part by it, Master Marner—'noculation, and everything to save it from harm—it 'ud be a thorn i' your bed forever o' this side the grave; and I can't think as it 'ud be easy lying down for anybody when they'd got to another world, if they hadn't done their part by the helpless children as come wi'out their own asking."

Dolly herself was disposed to be silent for some time now, for she had spoken from the depths of her own simple belief, and was much concerned to know whether her words would produce the desired effect on Silas. He was puzzled and anxious, for Dolly's word "christened" conveyed no distinct meaning to him. He had only heard of baptism, and had only seen the baptism of grown-up men and women.

"What is it as you mean by 'christened'?" he said at last, timidly. "Won't folks be good to her without it?"

"Dear, dear! Master Marner," said Dolly, with gentle distress and compassion. "Had you never no father nor mother as taught you to say your prayers, and as there's good words, and good things to keep us from harm?"

"Yes," said Silas, in a low voice; "I know a deal about that—used to, used to. But your ways are different: my country was a good way off." He paused a few moments, and then added, more decidedly, "But I want to do everything as can be done for the child. And whatever's right for it i' this country, and you think 'ull do it good, I'll act according, if you'll tell me."

"Well, then, Master Marner," said Dolly, inwardly rejoiced, "I'll ask Mr. Macey to speak to the parson about it and you fix on a name for it, because it must have a name giv' it when it's christened."

"My mother's name was Hephzibah," said Silas, "and my little sister was named after her."

"Eh, that's a hard name," said Dolly. "I partly think it isn't a christened name."

"It's a Bible name," said Silas, old ideas recurring.

"Then I've no call to speak again' it," said Dolly, rather startled by Silas's knowledge on this head; "but you see I'm no scholard, and I'm slow at catching the words. My husband says I'm allays like as if I was putting the haft for the handle—that's what he says—for he's very sharp, God help him. But it was awk'ard calling your little sister by such a hard name, when you'd got nothing big to say, like—wasn't it, Master Marner?"

"We called her Eppie," said Silas.

"Well, if it was noways wrong to shorten the name, it 'ud be a deal handier. And so I'll go now, Master Marner, and I'll speak about the christening afore dark; and I wish you the best o' luck, and it's my belief as it'll come to you, if you do what's right by the orphin child; and there's the 'noculation to be seen to; and as to washing its bits o' things, you need look to nobody but me, for I can do 'em wi' one hand when I've got my suds about. Eh, the blessed angil! You'll let me bring my Aaron one o' these days, and he'll show her his little cart as his father's made for him, and the black-and-white pup as he's got a-rearing."

Baby was christened, the rector deciding that a double baptism was a lesser risk to incur; and on this occasion Silas, making himself as clean and tidy as he could, appeared for the first time within the church, and shared in the observances held sacred by his neighbours. He was quite unable, by means of anything he heard or saw, to identify the Raveloe religion with his old faith; if he could at any time in his previous life have done so, it must have been by the aid of a strong feeling ready to vibrate with sympathy, rather than by a comparison of phrases and ideas: and now for long years that feeling had been dormant. He had no distinct idea about the baptism and the church-going, except that Dolly had said it was for the good of the child; and in this way, as the weeks grew to months, the child created fresh links between his life and the lives from which he had hitherto shrunk continually into narrower isolation. Unlike the gold which needed nothing, and must be worshipped in closelocked solitude—which was hidden away from the daylight, was deaf to the song of birds, and started to no human tones—Eppie was a creature of endless claims and ever-growing desires, seeking and loving sunshine, and living sounds, and living movements; making trial of everything, with trust in new joy, and stirring the human kindness in all eyes that looked on her. The gold had kept his thoughts in an ever-repeated circle, leading to nothing beyond itself; but Eppie was an object compacted of changes and hopes that forced his thoughts onward, and carried them far away from their old eager pacing towards the same blank limit—carried them away to new things that would come with the coming years, when Eppie would have learned to understand how her father Silas cared for her; and made him look for images of that time in the ties and charities that bound together the families of his neighbours. The gold had asked that he should sit weaving longer and longer, deafened and blinded more and more to all things except the monotony of his loom and the repetition of his web; but Eppie called him away from his weaving, and made him think all its pauses a holiday, reawakening his senses with her fresh life, even to the old winter flies that came crawling forth in the early spring sunshine, and warming him into joy because she had joy.

And when the sunshine grew strong and lasting, so that the buttercups were thick in the meadows, Silas might be seen in the sunny midday, or in the late afternoon when the shadows were lengthening under the hedgerows, strolling out with uncovered head to carry Eppie beyond the Stone Pits to where the flowers grew, till they reached some favourite bank where he could sit down, while Eppie toddled to pluck the flowers, and make remarks to the winged things that murmured happily above the bright petals, calling "Dad-dad's" attention continually by bringing him the flowers. Then she would turn her ear to some sudden bird note, and Silas learned to please her by making signs of hushed stillness, that they might listen for the note to come again: so that when it came, she set up her small back and laughed with gurgling triumph. Sitting on the banks in this way, Silas began to look for the once familiar herbs again; and as the leaves, with their unchanged outline and markings, lay on his palm, there was a sense of crowding remembrances from which he turned away timidly, taking refuge in Eppie's little world, that lay lightly on his enfeebled spirit.

As the child's mind was growing into knowledge, his mind was growing into memory: as her life unfolded, his soul, long stupefied in a cold, narrow prison, was unfolding too, and trembling gradually into full consciousness.

It was an influence which must gather force with every new year: the tones that stirred Silas's heart grew articulate, and called for more distinct answers; shapes and sounds grew clearer for Eppie's eyes and ears, and there was more that "Dad-dad" was imperatively required to notice and account for. Also, by the time Eppie was three years old, she developed a fine capacity for mischief, and for devising ingenious ways of being troublesome, which found much exercise, not only for Silas's patience, but for his watchfulness and penetration. Sorely was poor Silas puzzled on such occasions by the incompatible demands of love. Dolly Winthrop told him punishment was good for Eppie, and that, as for rearing a child without making it tingle a little in soft and safe places now and then, it was not to be done.

"To be sure, there's another thing you might do, Master Marner," added Dolly, meditatively: "you might shut her up once i' the coal hole. That was what I did wi' Aaron; for I was that silly wi' the youngest lad, as I could never bear to smack him. Not as I could find i' my heart to let him stay i' the coal hole more nor a minute, but it was enough to colly him all over, so as he must be new washed and dressed, and it was as good as a rod to him—that was. But I put it upo' your conscience, Master Marner, as there's one of 'em you must choose—ayther smacking or the coal hole—else she'll get so masterful, there'll be no holding her."

Silas was impressed with the melancholy truth of this last remark; but his force of mind failed before the only two penal methods open to him, not only because it was painful to him to hurt Eppie, but because he trembled at a moment's contention with her, lest she should love him the less for it. Let even an affectionate Goliath get himself tied to a small, tender thing, dreading to hurt it by pulling, and dreading still more to snap the cord, and which of the two, pray, will be master? It was clear that Eppie, with her short, toddling steps, must lead father Silas a pretty dance on any fine morning when circumstances favoured mischief.

For example. He had wisely chosen a broad strip of linen as a means of fastening her to his loom when he was busy: it made a broad belt round her waist, and was long enough to allow of her reaching to truckle bed and sitting down on it, but not long enough for her to attempt any dangerous climbing. One bright summer's morning Silas had been more engrossed than usual in "setting up" a new piece of work, an occasion on which his scissors were in requisition. These scissors, owing to an especial warning of Dolly's, had been kept carefully out of Eppie's reach; but the click of them had had a peculiar attraction for her ear, and watching the results of that click, she had derived the philosophic lesson that the same cause would produce the same effect. Silas had seated himself in his loom, and the noise of weaving had begun; but he had left his scissors on a ledge which Eppie's arm was long enough to reach; and now, like a small mouse, watching her opportunity, she stole quietly from her corner, secured the scissors, and toddled to the bed again, setting up her back as a mode of concealing the fact. She had a distinct intention as to the use of the scissors; and having cut the linen strip in a jagged but effectual manner, in two moments she had run out at the open door where the sunshine was inviting her, while poor Silas believed her to be a better child than usual. It was not until he happened to need his scissors that the terrible fact burst upon him: Eppie had run out by herself—had perhaps fallen into the Stone Pit. Silas, shaken by the worst fear that could have befallen him, rushed out, calling "Eppie!" and ran eagerly about the unenclosed space, exploring the dry cavities into which she might have fallen, and then gazing with questioning dread at the smooth red surface of the water. The cold drops stood on his brow. How long had she been out? There was one hope—that she had crept through the stile and got into the fields where he habitually took her to stroll. But the grass was high in the meadow, and there was no descrying her if she were there, except by a close search that would be a trespass on Mr. Osgood's crop. Still, that misdemeanour must be committed; and poor Silas, after peering all round the hedgerows, traversed the grass, beginning with perturbed vision to see Eppie behind every group of red

sorrel, and to see her moving always farther off as he approached. The meadow was searched in vain; and he got over the stile into the next field, looking with dying hope towards a small pond which was now reduced to its summer shallowness, so as to leave a wide margin of good adhesive mud. Here, however, sat Eppie, discoursing cheerfully to her own small boot, which she was using as a bucket to convey the water into a deep hoof mark, while her little naked foot was planted comfortably on a cushion of olive-green mud. A red-headed calf was observing her with alarmed doubt through the opposite hedge.

Here was clearly a case of aberration in a christened child which demanded severe treatment; but Silas, overcome with convulsive joy at finding his treasure again, could do nothing but snatch her up, and cover her with half-sobbing kisses. It was not until he had carried her home, and had begun to think of the necessary washing, that he recollected the need that he should punish Eppie, and "make her remember." The idea that she might run away again and come to harm gave him unusual resolution, and for the first time he determined to try the coal hole—a small closet near the hearth.

"Naughty, naughty Eppie," he suddenly began, holding her on his knee, and pointing to her muddy feet and clothes, "naughty to cut with the scissors and run away. Eppie must go into the coal hole for being naughty. Daddy must put her in the coal hole."

He half-expected that this would be shock enough, and that Eppie would begin to cry. But instead of that, she began to shake herself on his knee, as if the proposition opened a pleasing novelty. Seeing that he must proceed to extremities, he put her into the coal hole, and held the door closed, with a trembling sense that he was using a strong measure. For a moment there was silence, but then came a little cry, "Opy, opy!" and Silas let her out again, saying, "Now Eppie 'ull never be naughty again, else she must go in the coal hole—a black, naughty place."

The weaving must stand still a long while this morning, for now Eppie must be washed, and have clean clothes on; but it was to be hoped that this punishment would have a lasting effect, and save time in future—though, perhaps, it would have been better if Eppie had cried more.

In half an hour she was clean again, and Silas having turned his back to see what he could do with the linen band, threw it down again, with the reflection that Eppie would be good without fastening for the rest of the morning. He turned round again, and was going to place her in her little chair near the loom, when she peeped out at him with black face and hands again, and said, "Eppie in de toal hole!"

155

This total failure of the coal-hole discipline shook Silas's belief in the efficacy of punishment. "She'd take it all for fun," he observed to Dolly, "if I didn't hurt her, and that I can't do, Mrs. Winthrop. If she makes me a bit o' trouble, I can bear it. And she's got no tricks but what she'll grow out of."

"Well, that's partly true, Master Marner," said Dolly sympathetically, "and if you can't bring your mind to frighten her off touching things, you must do what you can to keep 'em out of her way. That's what I do wi' the pups as the lads are allays a-rearing. They will worry and gnaw—worry and gnaw they will, if it was one's Sunday cap as hung anywhere so as they could drag it. They know no difference, God help 'em; it's the pushing o' the teeth as sets 'em on, that's what it is."

So Eppie was reared without punishment, the burden of her misdeeds being borne vicariously by father Silas. The stone hut was made a soft nest for her, lined with downy patience; and also in the world that lay beyond the stone hut for her, she knew nothing of frowns and denials.

Notwithstanding the difficulty of carrying her and his yarn or linen at the same time, Silas took her with him in most of his journeys to the farmhouses, unwilling to leave her behind at Dolly Winthrop's, who was always ready to take care of her; and little curly-headed Eppie, the weaver's child, became an object of interest at several outlying homesteads, as well as in the village. Hitherto he had been treated very much as if he had been a useful gnome or brownie—a queer and unaccountable creature, who must necessarily be looked at with wondering curiosity and repulsion and with whom one would be glad to make all greetings and bargains as brief as possible, but who must be dealt with in a propitiatory way, and occasionally have a present of pork or garden stuff to carry home with him, seeing that without him there was no getting the yarn woven. But now Silas met with open smiling faces and cheerful questioning, as a person whose satisfactions and difficulties could be understood. Everywhere he must sit a little and talk about the child, and words of interest were always ready for him: "Ah, Master Marner, you'll be lucky if she takes the measles soon and easy!"—or, "Why, there isn't many lone men 'ud ha' been wishing to take up with a little un like that: but I reckon the weaving makes you handier than men as do outdoor work—you're partly as handy as a woman, for weaving comes next to spinning." Elderly masters and mistresses, seated observantly in large kitchen armchairs, shook their heads over the difficulties attendant on rearing children, felt Eppie's round arms and legs, and pronounced them remarkably firm, and told Silas that, if she turned out well (which, however, there was no telling), it would be a fine thing for him to have a steady lass to do for him when he got helpless. Servant maidens were fond of carrying her out to look at the hens and chickens, or to see if any cherries could be shaken down in the orchard; and the small boys and girls approached her slowly, with cautious movement and steady gaze, like little dogs face to face with one of their own kind, till attraction had reached the point at which the soft lips were put out for a kiss. No child was afraid of approaching Silas when Eppie was near him: there was no repulsion around him now, either for young or old: for the little child had come to link him once more with the whole world. There was love between him and the child that blent them into one, and there was love between the child and the world—from men and women with parental looks and tones, to the red lady-birds and the round pebbles.

Silas began now to think of Raveloe life entirely in relation to Eppie: she must have everything that was a good in Raveloe; and he listened docilely, that he might come to understand better what this life was, from which, for fifteen years, he had stood aloof as from a strange thing, with which he could have no communion: as some man who has a precious plant to which he would give a nurturing home in a new soil thinks of the rain and sunshine, and all influences, in relation to his nursling, and asks industriously for all knowledge that will help him to satisfy the wants of the searching roots, or to guard leaf and bud from invading harm. The disposition to hoard had been utterly crushed at the very first by the loss of his long-stored gold: the coins he earned afterwards seemed as irrelevant as stones brought to complete a house suddenly buried by an earthquake; the sense of bereavement was too heavy upon him for the old thrill of satisfaction to arise again at the touch of the newly earned coin. And now something had come to replace his hoard which gave a growing purpose to the earnings, drawing his hope and joy continually onward beyond the money.

In old days there were angels who came and took men by the hand and led them away from the city of destruction. We see no white-winged angels now. But yet men are led away from threatening destruction; a hand is put into theirs, which leads them forth gently towards a calm and bright land, so that they look no more backward; and the hand may be a little child's.

George Eliot

Jesus said, "Let the children come to me, and do not hinder them; for to such belongs the kingdom of heaven."

Matthew 19:14, Revised Standard Version

Considerate

If I can stop one heart from breaking,
I shall not live in vain;
If I can ease one life the aching,
Or cool one pain,
Or help one fainting robin
Unto his nest again,
I shall not live in vain.
I shall not live in vain.

Emily Dickinson

No one is useless in this world who lightens the burden of it to anyone
else.

Charles Dickens

THE GLOVE AND THE LIONS

King Francis was a hearty king, and loved a royal sport,
And one day, as his lions fought, sat looking on the court.
The nobles fill'd the benches, with the ladies in their pride,
And 'mongst them sat the Count de Lorge, with one for whom he sigh'd:
And truly 'twas a gallant thing to see that crowning show,
Valor and love, and a king above, and the royal beasts below.

Ramp'd and roar'd the lions, with horrid laughing jaws;
They bit, they glared, gave blows like beams, a wind went with their
    paws.
With wallowing might and stifled roar they roll'd on one another,
Till all the pit with sand and mane was in a thunderous smother;
The bloody foam above the bars came whicking through the air;
Said Francis then, "Faith, gentlemen, we're better here than there."

De Lorge's love o'erheard the king, a beauteous, lively dame,
With smiling lips and sharp bright eyes, which always seem'd the
    same;
She thought, The Count my lover is brave as brave can be;
He surely would do wondrous things to show his love of me;
King, ladies, lovers, all look on; the occasion is divine;
I'll drop my glove, to prove his love; great glory will be mine.

She dropp'd her glove, to prove his love, then look'd at him and smiled;
He bow'd and in a moment leaped among the lions wild:
The leap was quick, return was quick, he has regain'd his place,
Then threw the glove, but not with love, right in the lady's face.
"By heaven," said Francis, "rightly done!" and he rose from where
    he sat;
"No love," quote he, "but vanity, sets love a task like that."

Leigh Hunt

What is more gentle than a wind in summer?
John Keats

What do we live for, if it is not to make life less difficult to others?

George Eliot

The helping of man by man is God.
Thomas Carlyle

It is our daily duty to consider that in all circumstances of life, pleasurable, painful, or otherwise, the conduct of every human being affects, more or less, the happiness of others, especially of those in the same house; and that, as life is made up, for the most part, not of great occasions, but of small everyday moments, it is the giving to those moments their greatest amount of peace, pleasantness, and security, that contributes most to the sum of human good. Be peaceable. Be cheerful. Be true.

Leigh Hunt

LOVE CONSIDERS THE LOVED ONE *

The meaning of love concerns itself entirely with the loved one—with the way the loved one feels, with the way the loved one fares.

I intend to be as simple as possible here, because love is simple. Not simplistic. *Simple*. God has done all in his power to simplify love for us, even to coming in Person so that anyone—*anyone*—can learn something of the essence of his nature. This theme has saturated my thinking and my writing for nearly two decades. There will always be mystery, mystery about God himself, in all his infinite facets, mystery about the ongoing life after we leave this earth, mystery about death, even the death of a seed in the ground, which brings forth life

* Copyright © 1976 by Eugenia Price.

and growth. But the longer I live, the more convinced I become that mystery does not blot out the simplicity of God's motivation in love toward each one of us.

Nothing could be simpler than that "God is love." And yet, to millions, even to those who honestly seek to know him, God appears complex, as does love. But wait. Could it be that we confuse a holiness beyond our understanding, a power beyond anything we can conceive, a love so vast as to be incomprehensible, with *complexity?* Is it we who have caused God to appear complex? And, since "God is love," also complicated love itself? I do not mean the often brain-bending complexity of the learned theologian's dissertation on God. I speak of the ways in which we ourselves have decided *for* ourselves what love really is and then have tried to twist and bend God to fit that conception.

Love, *real* love, concerns itself always—not sometimes, but always—with the loved one, and never with the way the loved one is behaving or reacting.

I am writing this early in a new year and so I will use two very recent examples of what I mean; examples of love shown to me *not* because of any glorious way in which I was conducting myself, but because two people love me enough to care, first of all, how I feel. Not only do they love me enough, they love me as much as is humanly possible, with God's quality of love.

The first is my mother with whom I've just spent the Christmas holidays. I have been blessed by her rare caliber of giving love for all the years of my life, but this latest demonstration of unselfish love will stay with me. The night before I was to leave, we watched the superb final episode of *The Notorious Woman*, the life of the great French writer, George Sand—a woman who, when she found that her novels would not be published under her own name, changed both that name and her habits to those rather libertine ways which have more or less always been taken for granted in men. Now, the point of my story is not the morality or lack of it in the life of George Sand. But, considering the sheltered life Mother has lived, typical of her generation, I thought perhaps spots in the telecast might shock her. They did not. There, she is growing more and more like God, too, because he is (unlike most of us) not shockable. (Jesus Christ had to go to a cross because of human sin. He is not shocked, nor was he then, because he knows us exactly as we are.) No, Mother seemed to pay little or no attention to what George Sand had done. Rather, she was, like me, caught up in the absolutely magnificent artistry of Rosemary Harris, the actress who played the lead role. We were both transported.

As I said, we watched the performance the night before I had to fly out early the next day, perhaps not to see each other again for six months or so. When this is in print, Mother will be eighty years old and is very close to her daughter in mind and spirit. I experience her wrench along with my own every time we part. Any mother could be expected, I think, to shed a few tears and utter a few words of self pity (however well concealed) at such a moment. In fact, when I was dressing to come down to our last breakfast together for that visit, I wondered a bit how she'd be; as usual, I rather dreaded the finality.

Well, I'll tell you how she was. She was as magnificent as Rosemary Harris ever thought about being! As she came through the downstairs rooms toward the kitchen, where I'd already started our coffee brewing, she waved her cane dramatically, drew a deep, inspired breath and declared: "What a performance we saw last night! I woke up just now with my mind *filled* with George Sand!"

Instead of feeling slighted that my leaving did not fill her waking thoughts, my heart sang. We had grown still closer because of our mutual exhilaration from what we had seen together. I didn't need her expression of sadness. I already knew of her love. I needed what she was doing for me and I knew what she was doing. Not only did it make me love her more than ever, my admiration took a mighty leap, too. Here was a woman who knew *how* to love with the love of God, which *does* free us. And in freeing, draws us nearer. Her noble "performance" made me hate to leave her more than ever before, but my dread was gone. I had been shown love for my sake, not hers. I was freed to love her, unhooked completely from any shred of pity toward her. And pity, if it is on the human level, seldom frees.

The second example I want to share with you from recent experience has to do with another kind of human love, but one grounded in exactly the same kind of freeing devotion which God offers. This demonstration of selfless love went on from September through December 18 of last year when the great-hearted gentleman who showed this kind of love to me underwent radical surgery at our local hospital. His name is Mr. Johnnie Wilson, and my friend, Joyce Blackburn, and I have been blessed to have him look after us, our big yard and our house for almost a decade. Mr. Johnnie, after more than twenty years in responsible positions in New York, returned to his native St. Simons Island not long before we moved into our new house in the woods. He was on Social Security, but could work as much as we required considering the simplicity of our daily lives, and it was more than enough to spoil us forever! We retained him in the first place to care for the yard and to do the heavy work in the house. We hit it off, the three of us, in our humor, our political thinking and our personalities from the first meeting. I recall respecting the man so much for his innate intelligence and dignity that he had to call me to task after the initial few weeks for persisting in calling him Mr. Wilson. He brought his equally charming wife, Ruby, for a little visit during our first Christmas of sharing our lives and we have been Ruby-fans, too, ever since.

For a few months, Johnnie did the agreed amount of work for us with enormous care and judgment and sensitivity to our peculiar needs as writers. Then, before either Joyce or I realized it, *he* was adding things. Things such as building two new beautiful bird feeders for our brick wall out back—one with the initial "E" burned into the roof and the other with the initial "J". Next, he surprised us when we returned from a promotion tour with three equally craftsmanlike wooden bins built exactly to fit into the corner of our big wood box on the back porch—one smaller bin for sunflower seeds and two larger ones for cracked corn and wild bird seed. Before we realized it, Johnnie had begun to keep check on the contents of each bin and, finding them low, would stop at the grocery where we deal to keep the bins replenished. If we happened to be already at work when he got here in the morning, we knew the birds would be fed with the same tender, loving care we try to give them. Even to doughnuts for our temperamental mocker, crumbled on top of a certain post feeder, cracked corn in a particular place in the road that winds around our house and just the right amount of suet cake in just the right locations for the woodpeckers and catbirds. One day we discovered that Ruby, his wife, would not mind keeping our shirts and blouses in order, so for years all we've had to do is put a bundle on a wicker table on the porch and in a couple of days, Johnnie would come smiling, swinging hangers filled with clean, beautifully ironed shirts. Next, he got the idea that he could just as easily take our dry cleaning and bed linens to the Island Cleaners near his house. It is about a fifteen-mile drive to

and from the village from where we live, so he enabled us both to get to our typewriters as much as two hours early each day by adding to his list of love-gifts a cheerful offer to stop at the store where we buy meat and Tab and Fresca by the case. "Why should either one of you lug all those heavy cartons when I'm coming up anyway?" Why, indeed, when the man so obviously did all he did for us with *giving love.*

Perhaps the strongest bond of all among Johnnie, Joyce, Ruby and me is our mutual dependence on Jesus Christ. Johnnie and Ruby are people of enormous childlike faith and trust. More than once, Johnnie has reminded me of the lilies of the field when I've worked or worried myself into a bind over a deadline or a deluge of mail to be answered. Oh, that's another thing—he never left our lane without a handful of outgoing mail which he would take all the way to the Island post office, thereby getting it on its way a whole day sooner. When I could no longer step easily around my office for stacks of historical research material used for the most recent novel, it was Johnnie who took three truckloads of trash from my office to the Island dump. He became more than an integral part of our very daily lives.

And then one Sunday afternoon in September, as we sat relaxing on our back porch with a dear friend from New York, we heard Johnnie's car drive up the lane. He strode in, dressed to the nines, that melting smile lighting his handsome face, met our friend with his usual gallantry, and then, quite casually told us that Dr. Ben "wants to do a little snipping in my throat to see if there's any reason I keep having trouble with hiccups and swallowing." We knew he had dropped by to see Dr. Ben, but, at seventy, Johnnie had the body of a fifty-year-old, and serious illness was the furthest thing from our minds!

Of course, as people do, we talked all around the subject of a biopsy and tried to be gay and cheerful and hopeful, but Joyce and I were stunned to the depths of our beings. Johnnie told us two or three funny stories, checked on the bird seed, the Clorox and salt supply for our water conditioner, emptied the container of cans in the garage, and left us with a wave and a smile.

He had known for a week that he was entering the hospital the next day. He had seen no reason to worry us!

After an endless day or two, Dr. Ben's terrifying report to us meant long cobalt treatments to shrink the malignant growth in Johnnie's esophagus, then high-risk radical surgery to replace the esophagus.

Through more than three anxious weeks of daily cobalt treatments at the Brunswick Hospital on the mainland—except for two days when he felt ill by the time he had driven himself back across the marshes —Johnnie came to "work" *smiling*. We engaged his dependable cousin to care for our yard, which was still growing rampantly, but Johnnie kept up all his other love offerings to us—including re-doing the upstairs carpet because the job I'd done with the heavy vacuum cleaner did not suit him!

Then, just before Christmas, when we both were in deep conflict over leaving him to spend the holidays with our parents, he said, with that twinkle in his brown eyes: "Why do you ladies think I set the surgery for now? You've both been through enough worry over this thing. I'm not going to put you through that, too! Go on to your nice parents and don't worry about me. You're the ones always telling me that God is in charge—how about if I tell you the same thing right now? And don't give me any backtalk either!"

Johnnie has surprised even the doctors by making it through these first dangerous days. As soon as I returned from the holidays, I visited him in the intensive care unit at the hospital and he actually managed some of the old twinkle. In all the long days and nights of his violent suffering, he has managed to show that same giving love and patience to the nurses and doctors. They all will hate to see him go home, except that they have come to love him too and want only the best for the gentle, courageous, strong-spirited man. Three times he almost slipped into the "life after life." He will some day, as we all will, even if he comes out of this. But his quality of selfless love toward us has left us so aware of the intensive love of God that I'm finding (as is Joyce) less and less resistance within myself to all of life's prickly problems. I hear myself complaining less, adjusting more—almost without effort.

Oh, I'll work and fret myself into other binds over the mail, the outside drains on my energies, but I'll never forget the smile and the encouragement *toward us* on the warm, brown face of this man who concerned himself about us while facing the distinct possibility of his own death. If Johnnie's loving concern has so changed me, how can we be amazed at the changing power of the love of God?

Johnnie was afraid of the suffering that lay ahead. He's human. He didn't want to leave Ruby or us. He loved his work with us, but he loved us more—enough, as did God, to give himself in his own time of desperate need. Of course, we've tried to give to him of ourselves, too, but he has inspired what little we could give by concerning himself first with how we felt.

I try to give to Mother, too, but her lifetime of giving to me has taught me *how*. In my heart, I know how much she hates to see me leave each time—I haven't lived at home since I was fifteen. She has spent her life saying goodbye to her only daughter, but this time she topped even her own past performances. She didn't dread my leaving any less, but she is learning, as her daughter is learning, more and more about the true *meaning of love*.

The kind of love that concerns itself first for the loved one.

Eugenia Price

Everything

ALL FOR LOVE

O talk not to me of a name great in story;
The days of our youth are the days of our glory;
And the myrtle and ivy of sweet two-and-twenty
Are worth all your laurels, though ever so plenty.
What are garlands and crowns to the brow that is wrinkled?
'Tis but as a dead flower with May-dew besprinkled;
Then away with all such from the head that is hoary—
What care I for the wreaths that can only give glory?
Oh Fame!—if I e'er took delight in thy praises,
'Twas less for the sake of thy high-sounding phrases,
Than to see the bright eyes of the dear one discover
She thought that I was not unworthy to love her.
There chiefly I sought thee, there only I found thee!
Her glance was the best of the rays that surround thee,
When it sparkled o'er aught that was bright in my story,
I knew it was love, and I felt it was glory.

George Gordon, Lord Byron

From REASONS FOR CONSTANCY

Not, Celia, that I juster am,
  Or better than the rest!
For I would change each hour like them,
  Were not my heart at rest.

But I am tied to very thee
  By every thought I have;
Thy face I only care to see,
  Thy heart I only crave.

All that in woman is adored
  In thy dear self I find;
For the whole sex can but afford
  The handsome and the kind.

Why then should I seek further store
  And still make love anew?
When change itself can give no more,
  'Tis easy to be true.
                    Sir Charles Sedley

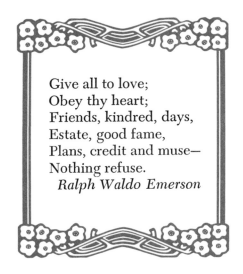

Give all to love;
Obey thy heart;
Friends, kindred, days,
Estate, good fame,
Plans, credit and muse—
Nothing refuse.
  Ralph Waldo Emerson

When, in disgrace with fortune and men's eyes,
I all alone beweep my outcast state
And trouble deaf heaven with my bootless cries
And look upon myself and curse my fate,
Wishing me like to one more rich in hope,
Featured like him, like him with friends possessed,
Desiring this man's art and that man's scope,
With what I most enjoy contented least;
Yet in these thoughts myself almost despising,
Haply I think on thee, and then my state,
Like to the lark at break of day arising
From sullen earth, sings hymns at heaven's gate;
  For thy sweet love remembered such wealth brings
  That then I scorn to change my state with kings.
William Shakespeare

To love very much is to love inadequately;
we love—that is all.

Love cannot be modified without being
nullified. Love is a short word but it contains
everything.

Love means the body, the soul, the life, the
entire being.

We feel love as we feel the warmth of our blood,
we breathe love as we breathe the air, we hold it in
ourselves as we hold our thoughts. Nothing more
exists for us.

Love is not a word; it is a wordless state indicated
by four letters. . . .

Guy de Maupassant

How do I love thee? Let me count the ways.
I love thee to the depth and breadth and height
My soul can reach, when feeling out of sight
For the ends of Being and ideal Grace.
I love thee to the level of every day's
Most quiet need, by sun and candlelight.
I love thee freely, as men strive for Right;
I love thee purely, as they turn from Praise.
I love thee with the passion put to use
In my old griefs, and with my childhood's faith.
I love thee with a love I seemed to lose
With my lost saints, —I love thee with the breath,
Smiles, tears, of all my life!—and, if God choose,
I shall but love thee better after death.

Elizabeth Barrett Browning

He who loves can never want. The universe belongs to Goodness, and it therefore belongs to the good man. It can be possessed by all without stint of shrinking, for Goodness, and the abundance of Goodness (material, mental, and spiritual abundance) is inexhaustible. Think lovingly, speak lovingly, act lovingly, and your every need shall be supplied; you shall not walk in desert places, . . . no danger shall overtake you.

James Allen

If we love one another, nothing, in truth, can harm us, whatever mischances may happen.

Henry Wadsworth Longfellow

Love suffereth long, and is kind; love envieth not; love vaunteth not itself, is not puffed up,

Doth not behave itself unseemly, seeketh not her own, is not easily provoked, thinketh no evil;

Rejoiceth not in iniquity, but rejoiceth in the truth;

Beareth all things, believeth all things, hopeth all things, endureth all things.

Love never faileth. . . .

And now abideth faith, hope, love, these three; but the greatest of these is love.

I Corinthians 13:4–8, 13, King James Version

APPROACHES

When thou turn'st away from ill,
Christ is this side of thy hill.

When thou turnest toward good,
Christ is walking in thy wood.

When thy heart says, "Father, pardon!"
Then the Lord is in thy garden.

When stern Duty wakes to watch,
Then His hand is on the latch.

But when Hope thy song doth rouse,
Then the Lord is in the house.

When to love is all thy wit,
Christ doth at thy table sit.

When God's will is thy heart's pole,
Then is Christ thy very soul.

George MacDonald

The grand essentials to happiness in this life are something to do, something to love and something to hope for.

Joseph Addison

> Take away love, and our earth is a tomb.
> *Robert Browning*

Brothers, love the whole of God's creation, all of it down to the very dust. Love each leaf, each ray of God's light, love animals, love plants, love everything. If you love everything, you will understand the mystery of God in things. Once you see this, you will go on understanding it better every day. And eventually you will love the world with a love that includes every single thing. Love animals: God has given them a kind of thought and a tranquil enjoyment. Do not disturb it, do not hurt them, do not spoil their happiness, do not go contrary to God's purposes for them. Love little children especially, for they are innocent as angels; they are given to us as a sign, to touch and cleanse our hearts.

Feodor Dostoevski

LOVE COMES FIRST IN CREATIVE LIVING *

The title, *Love Comes First in Creative Living*, really understates the theme, for indeed love comes first in everything. Without love, you are nothing, I am nothing, the world is nothing. If it were possible to sum up the teachings of Christianity in one word, that word would be *love*.

"A new commandment I give unto you," said Jesus to His disciples at the Last Supper, "that ye love one another; as I have loved you, that ye also love one another." And the Apostle John years later, when he was an aged man, gathered the people around him and told them to love one another.

Some people mistake Christianity for a system of rules: you shouldn't do this, you shouldn't do that; you must do this, you must do that. But what some interpret as rules is only what man had added. In its beginnings, in its essence, in the simple teachings of Jesus, Christianity is a religion of love. That is basic.

* Used by permission of The Foundation for Christian Living, Pawling, New York.

175

And this emphasis on love is not only for the purpose of making a better world, although a better world will come when we truly love one another. The primary reason for the Gospel stressing love is that a person will actually wither and die ultimately unless he has love in his heart, both for himself and toward other people. One of the greatest books on this subject to appear in many years was written by the late Smiley Blanton, with whom I had the honor to found the American Foundation of Religion and Psychiatry. Smiley Blanton was one of the great American psychiatrists of our day, one of the great teachers, one of the great lovers of humanity. He wrote a book entitled *Love or Perish*. Either you love or you will perish.

Here is one thought-provoking passage from the beginning of that book: "To say that one will perish without love does not mean that everyone without adequate love dies. Many do, for without love the will to live is often impaired to such an extent that a person's resistance is critically lowered and death follows. But most of the time, lack of love makes people depressed, anxious, and without zest for life. They remain lonely and unhappy, without friends or work they care for, their life a barren treadmill, stripped of all creative action and joy." Love or perish! No wonder Jesus makes love central to His whole teaching! If you are going to live and live creatively, you must learn to love.

In the youth movements of today there is a religious emphasis which the young people say is deepened as they share, they touch, they communicate. They try to draw together, claiming that the civilization in which they were reared has thrust them apart. Of course, some of these movements need to be better balanced, but the emphasis on fellowship and love is so necessary.

A judge in Philadelphia, speaking of his experience in dealing with juveniles in trouble with the law, said that most of the young people who came before his court for discipline were very hostile and very aggressive, but their attitude didn't bother him nearly so much as the attitude of their parents. Often the father would be outraged: "Why do you do this to my boy?" he would ask. "Why bring him in here? Don't you know who I am?"

"But," said the judge, "never once did I see any of those fathers show any sign of affection for their teenagers. Never once did a father put his arm around his son or daughter. Never once did he even touch his child. When a parent will show love, even by a simple act of touching, there is an opportunity for redemption. Otherwise, young people die emotionally, they die mentally, they die in their personalities because of a lack of love."

Now in order to avoid misunderstandings when talking about love, you must define it. The kind of love I am talking about is not the kind that is dished up by Hollywood. Neither is it the kind that revolves around romantic relationships. Of course, romantic love has its place in life, but it doesn't need any extra emphasis. It gets along pretty well on its own! The kind of love we mean is a deep feeling for others, for people generally, that is hard to express. If you are part of a group trying to seek understanding and help, you can experience communication by a smile, by a handshake, by a pat on the shoulder or on the back. It transmits a feeling that cannot easily be put into words. How do you express love? By sharing, by touching, by approximation to one another.

I think one of the most moving stories I ever heard in my life is one that came out of World War I—which is now so far back in time that perhaps only a few of us remember it. It is about two brothers. And I knew these two brothers. They hadn't seen each other for many months—from the time they left home to go across the sea and into Flanders. Then one night some men coming out of the trenches passed a detachment of men coming in to replace them and all of a sudden in the light of the moon these two brothers came face to face with each other, one going into the trenches, the other coming out.

Now how would you think two soliders, brothers, meeting each other for a moment under circumstances where the danger of death was constantly hanging over them—how would you think they would greet each other? They didn't say a word. They didn't ask, "How is Mom?" or "How is Dad?" or "How is Mary?" or "How is Genevieve?" or anything of the sort. They started punching each other, like they were boxing! The punches thudded from chest to chest. Then one said to the other, "See you, boy." The other said, "See you, kid." And they separated.

Men standing by understood. This was love in its deepest expression. Girls might embrace. Men punch each other. But all who saw it were uplifted by it and trudged on up or down the trench brushing tears from their eyes.

Love comes first in creative living . . . and in order to have it you must love yourself. That is primary. That is the first thing that should be said: Love yourself. Do you love yourself?

"Oh," you say, "that's easy. I sure do like myself. I am very proud of myself."

But wait a minute. That isn't love. That is egotism. True love of yourself is having a deep, joyous respect for yourself, being mindful of your God-given abilities and capabilities and potentials and using them to the fullest extent.

The Gospel indicates that without this wholesome, loving respect for yourself you cannot really love anybody else. It tells us, "Thou shalt love thy neighbor as thyself." This implies that if you don't love yourself you won't love your neighbor. But if you do love and respect yourself as a child of God, then you can likewise love and respect the other fellow as a child of God.

One time a man came to see me because he couldn't get along with anybody in his office. He fought with his subordinates all the time. He yelled at them, he made scenes. He threw his weight around. And he said to me, "I know I shouldn't act like this. I am supposed to be an administrator. I am no good as an administrator. I haven't got what it takes. I am an awful failure!"

Well, we went into the problem and found that his trouble was largely due to two women. One was his mother. She was a dominating woman and had dominated him from the day he was born. She supervised him; she called the shots; she told him exactly what he could do and what he couldn't do; she directed his every action. He was supine and yielded, but he got to hating her. Then he had guilt feelings.

178

Presently there came the time when he said to himself, "I am now twenty-one and I'll get married and get away from my mother." But you have to be very careful! Because he married a girl who looked sweet, innocent, soft and inoffensive, but was inwardly the spit and image of his mother. And she began to supervise him, dominate him, direct him.

So what could the poor fellow do but go to the office and throw his weight around by way of getting psychologically as far away as possible from this domination by two women who loved him, but over-loved him. Well, all that was necessary was to explain to him this mechanism of his unconscious mind and help him to realize that as a child of God he had within him the power and capacity to overcome it and completely change his personality. When he understood this, I said to him, "If I were you, I would take charge of both of them." (Meaning wife and mother.)

"Do you think I could?" he asked.

"You go to it," I said. "I'll be right behind you—at a safe distance!"

So he began to treat the mother not as a mother but as a woman and the wife not as a wife but as a woman and he rapidly developed normal respect for himself. When he did, he loved the two women more, both mother and wife; and they loved him more—and increasingly he was able to relate to the people in his business life on a basis of mutual regard and good will.

So if you do not have this healthy spiritual self-esteem, by all means seek to have it. Pray about it, read the Bible, get closer to God. You will automatically learn to love yourself as you become increasingly aware of God's everlasting, unremitting, constant love for you.

One of the greatest statements ever made is this: "For God so loved the world, that he gave his only begotten Son, that whosoever believeth in him should not perish, but have everlasting life." If you were called upon to demonstrate love, what greater example could you give than this? It's the most poignant gift of love ever known in all the history of mankind. Its culmination was the crucifixion.

After scourging Jesus, putting a crown of thorns on His head, laughing Him to scorn, spitting on Him, showing Him every contempt, the Roman soldiers nailed Him to a cross. Then, raising the cross, they let it fall into the earth with a thud. It must have pulled on every tendon and every muscle with excruciating pain. And Jesus, in body, was human. Yet as He hung there, what did He say? "Father, forgive them; for they know not what they do." What greater love could there be?

There is no circumstance in your life where God will not stand with you and help you, no matter what it is. He understands all your troubles, all your frustrations and disappointments. He understands your weaknesses. He loves you.

Recently my wife and I rode with a taxi driver who proved to be a very interesting man. His name written on the license was Dutch and I asked if he was from Europe.

"Yes," he said, "from Rotterdam."

"Well," I replied, "I happen to be minister of the old Dutch Reformed Church in New York."

"Oh," he commented in surprise, "then you're Dr. Peale."

"Yes, sir," I said.

"I've been to your church," he continued, "but I didn't recognize you without your robe."

"Yes," I said, "there is a difference between a gown and a business suit." And we had a nice little chat.

As we drove along he asked, "Have you time to let me tell you a little story? It is about the time I met God, and it shows how good God is. I have great faith, sir, and I know that I can never get outside the care and love of God.

"It was close to the end of the war and I was a little boy. Our country had been ravaged. The conquerors had been driven out, but we were left absolutely destitute. We had ration stamps, but they weren't any good, for we had no food at all. There was no food in the warehouses or in the stores or in the country districts. Holland had been swept clean of foodstuffs."

"We were reduced to eating beets out of the fields and it was a kind of beet that is dangerous to eat without long cooking—and even then if you don't accompany it with other food the chemical reaction will bloat and distend the stomach. People have been known to die from the chemical which they absorbed from an overdose." He continued, "You know how beautiful Holland tulips are? We dug the bulbs out of the ground and ate them. That was all we had. We were desperate.

"Then a notice from our pastor went around, telling us that there would be a meeting in the church; that, since we were reduced to the final circumstances, we would have a meeting and pray to God and tell Him we are His children and ask Him to feed us. It was the only hope we had. The big church was packed; two thousand people were present. There was no sermon. We prayed for an hour or two. The pastor prayed. People prayed aloud all over the church. We sat there herded together, praying to God.

"I was only a little boy, but all of a sudden I became aware that God was right there and I was almost frightened. I could feel Him in my heart. I knew that He was present and I knew that He was going to take care of us poor starving people.

"Then we sang one of those old Dutch hymns of faith and we went out to the streets and to our homes; and with gnawing, empty stomach I fell asleep. Early the next morning we were awakened by the roar of a great armada of airplanes over Rotterdam and there began a shower of food. It seemed that the sky was full of packages of food floating down to the streets of Rotterdam, filling the avenues with fine food. And we ate. And we were saved."

He glanced back at us from the driver's seat as he said, "As long as I live I will believe that God heard those prayers, and out of His great heart of love He fed his children."

And so do I believe it. And I am sure you do also. He is a loving God. He loves you more dearly than your mother loves you or your father. You are His child. So just get to know Him and trust His love. Then you will have that wholesome esteem for your own self which leads to having a respect and love for all people.

The next thing is to make loving your neighbor a conscious daily practice. In a huge city people come at you by the thousands. On the streets there are so many that it bewilders you, and, when you are crowded into subways or fast-moving buses or trains with so many others, it often seems insufferable. But Jesus Christ said that we should love one another. So if you and I want to live creatively and grow in spirit we must practice loving people, not as groups of people, but individually, in Jesus' name. And if each of us, loving himself as a child of God and loving Jesus, would really begin loving all people as our neighbors, why, we would change the atmosphere of the world in no time.

Without love we are nothing. The Bible tells us, "I may have all knowledge and understand all secrets; I may have all the faith needed to move mountains—but if I have not love, I am nothing. I may give away everything I have, and even give up my body to be burned—but if I have not love, it does me no good. Love is patient and kind; love is not jealous, or conceited, or proud; love is not ill-mannered, or selfish, or irritable; love does not keep a record of wrongs; love is not happy with evil, but is happy with the truth. Love never gives up: its faith, hope, and patience never fail. Love is eternal." (*Good News for Modern Man—The New Testament in Today's English Version*).

Norman Vincent Peale

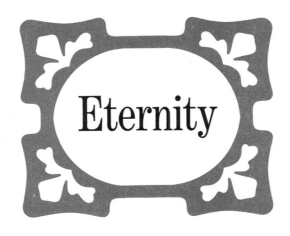

Eternity

LOVE IS OF GOD

Beloved, let us love: love is of God;
In God alone hath love its true abode.

Beloved, let us love: for they who love,
They only, are His sons, born from above.

Beloved, let us love: for love is rest,
And he who loveth not dwelleth in night.

Beloved, let us love: for only thus
Shall we behold that God who loveth us.
Horatius Bonar

IN SWEET COMMUNION

May the grace of Christ our Saviour, and the Father's boundless love,
With the Holy Spirit's favor, rest upon us from above.
Thus may we abide in union with each other and the Lord,
And possess in sweet communion joys which earth cannot afford.
John Newton

REMEMBER THESE WORDS

We are gathered together
    on this happy day
To stand before God and to reverently say:
    I take thee to be my partner
      for life,
    To love and to live with
      as husband and wife;
To have and to hold forever, Sweetheart,
    Through sickness and health
      until death do us part;
To love and to cherish whatever betide,
    And in BETTER or WORSE
      to stand by your side. . . .
We do this not lightly but solemnly, Lord,
    Asking Thy blessing
      as we live in accord
    With THY HOLY PRECEPTS which
      join us in love
    And assure us Thy guidance
      and grace from above. . . .
    And grant us, dear Lord, that
      "I WILL" and "I DO"
    Are words that grow deeper
      and more meaningful, too,
Through long happy years of caring
      and sharing,
    Secure in the knowledge
      that we are preparing
A love that is endless and never
      can die
But finds its fulfillment with YOU
      in the "SKY."

Helen Steiner Rice

AN EPITAPH

To these whom death again did wed
This grave's the second marriage-bed.
For though the hand of Fate could force
'Twixt soul and body a divorce,
It could not sever man and wife,
Because they both lived but one life.
Peace, good reader, do not weep;
Peace, the lovers are asleep.
They, sweet turtles, folded lie
In the last knot that love could tie.
Let them sleep, let them sleep on,
Till the stormy night be gone,
And the eternal morrow dawn;
Then the curtains will be drawn,
And they wake into a light
Whose day shall never die in night.

Richard Crashaw

That I did always love,
    I bring thee proof;
That till I loved
    I did not love enough.

That I shall love alway,
    I offer thee
That love is life,
    And life hath immortality.

This, dost thou doubt, sweet?
    Then have I
Nothing to show
    But Calvary.

Emily Dickinson

For there are two heavens, sweet,
    Both made of love, —one, inconceivable
Ev'n by the other, so divine it is;
The other, far on this side of the stars,
By men called home.

Leigh Hunt

EASTER HYMN

Christ the Lord is risen today,
    Sons of men and angels say:
Raise your joys and triumphs high,
    Sing, ye heavens, and earth reply.

Love's redeeming work is done,
    Fought the fight, the battle won;
Lo! our Sun's eclipse is o'er;
    Lo! He sets in blood no more.

Vain the stone, the watch, the seal;
    Christ hath burst the gates of hell!
Death in vain forbids His rise;
    Christ hath opened Paradise!

Loves again our glorious King:
    Where, O Death, is now they sting?
Once He died, our souls to save:
    Where thy victory, O Grave?

Charles Wesley

In the beginning was the Word, and the Word was with God, and the Word was God. He was in the beginning with God; all things were made through him, and without him was not anything made that was made. In him was life, and the life was the light of men. The light shines in the darkness, and the darkness has not overcome it.

There was a man sent from God, whose name was John. He came for testimony, to bear witness to the light, that all might believe through him. He was not the light, but came to bear witness to the light.

The true light that enlightens every man was coming into the world. He was in the world, and the world was made through him, yet the world knew him not. He came to his own home, and his own people received him not. But to all who received him, who believed in his name, he gave power to become children of God; who were born, not of blood nor of the will of the flesh nor of the will of man, but of God.

And the Word became flesh and dwelt among us, full of grace and truth; we have beheld his glory, glory as of the only Son from the Father. . . . And from his fulness have we all received, grace upon grace. For the law was given through Moses; grace and truth came through Jesus Christ. No one has ever seen God; the only Son, who is in the bosom of the Father, he has made him known.

John 1:1–18, Revised Standard Version

I SOUGHT THE LORD

I sought the Lord, and afterward I knew
He moved my soul to seek Him, seeking me;
It was not I that found, O Saviour true,
No, I was found of Thee.

Thou didst reach forth Thy hand and mine enfold;
I walked and sank not on the storm-vexed sea,—
'Twas not so much that I on Thee took hold,
As Thou, dear Lord, on me.

I find, I walk, I love, but, O the whole
Of love is but my answer, Lord, to Thee:
For Thou wert long beforehand with my soul,
Always Thou lovedst me.

Author unknown

Christ be with me, Christ within me,
Christ behind me, Christ before me,
Christ beside me, Christ to win me,
Christ to comfort and restore me,
Christ beneath me, Christ above me,
Christ in quiet, Christ in danger,
Christ in hearts of all that love me,
Christ in mouth of friend and stranger.

St. Patrick

WHAT IS LOVE?

 What is love?
No words can define it,
It's something so great
Only God could design it. . . .
    Wonder of Wonders,
    Beyond man's conception,
    And only in God
    Can love find true perfection,

188

For love means much more
Than small words can express,
For what man calls love
Is so very much less

Than the beauty and depth
And the true richness of
God's gift to mankind—
His compassionate love. . . .
For love has become
A word that's misused,
Perverted, distorted
And often abused,
To speak of "light romance"
Or some affinity for
A passing attraction
That is seldom much more
Than a mere interlude
Of inflamed fascination,
A romantic fling
Of no lasting duration . . .
But love is enduring
And patient and kind,
It judges all things
With the heart, not the mind,
And love can transform
The most commonplace
Into beauty and splendor
And sweetness and grace. . . .
For love is unselfish,
Giving more than it takes,
And no matter what happens
Love never forsakes,
It's faithful and trusting
And always believing,
Guileless and honest
And never deceiving. . . .
Yes, love is beyond
What man can define,
For love is immortal
And God's Gift is Divine!

Helen Steiner Rice

Divine

FATHER, HOW WIDE THY GLORIES SHINE

Father, how wide thy glories shine,
God of the universe, and mine!
Thy goodness watches o'er the whole,
As all mankind were but one soul,
Yet keeps my every sacred hair,
As I remain'd thy single care.

Charles Wesley

THE LOVE OF GOD *

Human love is an awesomely wonderful thing. It can weld two humans together in the joyous bonds of marriage. It can form the strong ties of family relations—parent and child, brother and sister. It can bind human beings together in mutual brotherhood and friendship that can be lifelong.

But there is a greater love than human love—the love of God. Human love is often changeable; God's love never changes. Human love is often tinged with selfishness; God's love is completely selfless. Human love is limited; God's love knows no bounds. Human love at

* Copyright © 1976 by Billy Graham.

190

best is still imperfect; God's love is always perfect. We love some people because we find them loveable; God loves even the unlovely, even those who hate Him.

God's love is seen in many ways. It is seen first of all in God's creation of this wonderful world in which we live. God did not have to make the heavens vast and beautiful—but He did. God did not have to make the blazing color of the autumn leaves or the quiet music of a mountain stream—but He did. God did not even have to create us with the ability to appreciate the beauty of His creation—but He did, because He loves us. "Every good gift and every perfect gift is from above, and cometh down from the Father of lights, with whom there is no variableness, neither shadow of turning" (James 1:17).

God's love is also seen in the way He cares for us day by day. The food we eat, the air we breathe, the natural resources we use to sustain our lives and to bring us comfort, come ultimately from the hands of our loving God. Yes, it is true that sin has warped this world, and it is true that human sin continues to distort the world. Our sin blinds us to our dependence upon God, and we do not thank God for His provision. But all we have, and all we are, is possible only because God in His love continues to sustain our lives.

The greatest expression of God's love, however, is more awesome and more wonderful to me than the love He has shown us in creating us and sustaining us. The greatest expression of God's love is that He sent His only Son into the world, to give us salvation. "In this was manifested the love of God toward us, because that God sent his only begotten Son into the world, that we might live through him" (I John 4:9).

The Bible tells us that there is something tragically wrong with the human race. We were created for perfect fellowship with God. We were meant to live for Him and to trust Him for everything. However, man rebelled against God and chose to go his own way apart from God. The Bible calls this rebellion "sin," and tells us that it has brought untold suffering and misery to the human race. Even death—which none of us can escape—has come to us ultimately because of our rebellion against God.

But God still loves us! We have done everything imaginable to incur His wrath, but in spite of this God has not given up on us. The Bible tells us that "before the foundation of the world" (I Peter 1:20) God chose His Son, Jesus Christ, to come to earth and bring us back into a right relationship with God. Throughout history God has been seeking man, and this is why Christ came. "For the Son of man is come to seek and to save that which was lost" (Luke 19:10).

I cannot understand it fully. There is no logical reason for it. And yet God loved me so much—He loves you so much—that He sent His Son to die on the cross for our sins. I deserved to die on that rough Roman cross. But the sinless Son of God took my place and suffered the pangs of death and judgment for me. "For when we were yet without strength, in due time Christ died for the ungodly. For scarcely for a righteous man will one die: yet peradventure for a good man some would even dare to die. But God commendeth his love toward us, in that, while we were yet sinners, Christ died for us" (Romans 5:6–8).

Do you want to know if God loves you? Don't look just at this world He has created, wonderful as it is. Don't just look at the way He has taken care of you in the past. Look at the Cross! "For God so loved the world, that he gave his only begotten Son, that whosoever believeth in him should not perish, but have everlasting life" (John 3:16).

What should be our response to the love of God?

First, our response must be one of faith and trust. The love of God is not simply a nice thought to be stored away in our memories. It is not just a theological concept to which we give mental assent. It demands instead the commitment of our whole lives to God. By faith in Christ we can know forgiveness and joy and hope. By faith and trust in Him we can know that nothing "shall be able to separate us from the love of God, which is in Christ Jesus our Lord" (Romans 8:39).

Second, our response should be one of thankfulness and love toward God. "Be thankful unto him, and bless his name. For the Lord is good; his mercy is everlasting; and his truth endureth to all generations" (Psalm 100:4, 5). Jesus said, "Thou shalt love the Lord thy God with all thy heart, and with all thy soul, and with all thy mind" (Matthew 22:37).

Third, our response should be one of obedience to God. When we come to know Christ, we have a new Master over us. He died for us— let us live for Him! "He that hath my commandments, and keepeth them, he it is that loveth me" (John 14:21).

Fourth, our response should be love toward others. By nature we are selfish, and at best our love of others is imperfect. When we come to Christ, however, God by His Holy Spirit gives us a new ability to love.

"But the fruit of the Spirit is love" (Galatians 5:22). We need to pray for more of this love, and to ask God to show us practical ways of expressing love to others. We are to have this same kind of self-sacrificing love which Christ had when He "took upon him the form of a servant, and . . . humbled himself, and became obedient unto death, even the death of the cross" (Philippians 2:7, 8). There are many ways of expressing the love of God to others, but certainly the greatest way is telling others of the One who loves them and wants them to come to faith, thankfulness, obedience, and love as they commit their lives to Christ.

Yes, God loves us with an eternal and boundless love. Let us trust that love, and let us live our lives as children of our loving Heavenly Father.

Billy Graham

Indexes

TITLES AND FIRST LINES

A gentle boy, with soft and silken locks, 83

A hermit's house beside a stream, 75

Ah! What would the world be to us, 73

ALL FOR LOVE, 168

ALL-EMBRACING, THE, 70

Am I a stone, and not a sheep, 64

And what is a kiss, when all is done? 84

And when with grief you see your brother stray, 69

ANNABEL LEE, 87

Apple orchards, the trees all covered with blossoms, 109

APPROACHES, 174

AS THRO' THE LAND AT EVE WE WENT, 53

BABY, 54

BALLAD OF TREES AND THE MASTER, A, 69

Batter my heart, three person'd God; for, you, 68

Be useful where thou livest, that they may, 99

Behold, how good and pleasant it is, 58

Beloved, let us love: love is of God, 183

Blessed is every one who fears the Lord, 57

Breathes there a man with soul so dead, 75

BY THE SEA, 22

CARE AND FEEDING OF GRANDPARENTS, THE, 14

CASTLE-BUILDER, THE, 83

CENTENNIAL ODE, THE, 116

Christ be with me, Christ within me, 188

Christ the Lord is risen today, 186

COMFORT, 101

COMPLEAT ANGLER, THE, 59

DIFFERENCE BETWEEN ROMANCE AND LOVE, THE, 91

EASTER HYMN, 186

EPITAPH, AN, 185

ETERNAL GOODNESS, THE, 103

Farewell to the Highlands, farewell to the North, 74

FATHER, HOW WIDE THY GLORIES SHINE, 190

FIRST DAY, THE, 89

For there are two heavens, sweet, 186

Give all to love, 169

GLOVE AND THE LIONS, THE, 160

GOOD FRIDAY, 64

GOOD MORROW, THE, 90

GRIEF, 135

He jests at scars, that never felt a wound, 88

He loved me well, 76

He that loves a rosy cheek, 108

He who bestows his goods upon the poor, 76

Hither thou com'st: the busy wind all night, 21

How do I love thee? Let me count the ways, 173

How long it is since she with whom I lay, 18

I am content with what I have, 57

I come not to ASK, to PLEAD or IMPLORE You, 21

I had no time to hate, because, 25

I lived with visions for my company, 109

I said, "Let me walk in the field," 44

I SAW IN LOUISIANA A LIVE-OAK GROWING, 24

I see the wrong that round me lies, 103

I SOUGHT THE LORD, 188

I sought the Lord, and afterward I knew, 188

I will lift up mine eyes unto the hills, 106

I wish I could remember the first day, 89

I wonder by my troth, what thou and I, 90

If I can stop one heart from breaking, 159

If thou wouldst learn, not knowing how to pray, 23

If yet I have not all thy love, 32

In a world where, 22

IN SWEET COMMUNION, 183

Indeed this very love which is my boast, 31

Into the woods my Master went, 69

Is this a Fast, to keep, 63

It is a beauteous evening, calm and free, 22

It takes a GROOM, 50

It was many and many a year ago, 87

King Francis was a hearty king, and loved a royal sport, 160

Know you the land where the lemon-trees bloom, 90

Let me but live my life from year to year, 57

Let me not to the marriage of true minds, 27

Like the ghost of a dear friend dead, 17

LITTLE WOMEN, 35

LOCHINVAR, 93

Long as thine art shall love true love, 116

LOVE BADE ME WELCOME, 65

Love bade me welcome; yet my soul drew back, 65

LOVE COMES FIRST IN CREATIVE LIVING, 175

LOVE CONSIDERS THE LOVED ONE, 161

LOVE IS OF GOD, 183

LOVE IS SOMETHING YOU DO, 77

LOVE OF GOD, THE, 190

May the grace of Christ our Saviour, and the Father's boundless love, 183

MERCHANT OF VENICE, THE, 70

My good blade carries the casques of men, 104

MY HEART'S IN THE HIGHLANDS, 74

My letters! all dead paper, mute and white! 92

MY TRUE LOVE HATH MY HEART, 112

My true love hath my heart, and I have his, 112

Nature is but a name for an effect, 109

NATURE OF PERSECUTION, THE, 43

NEW COLOSSUS, THE, 101

NO FAVOR DO I SEEK TODAY, 21

NO TIME LIKE THE OLD TIME, 19

Not, Celia, that I juster am, 169

Not like the brazen giant of Greek fame, 101

O talk not to me of a name great in story, 168

Oh the brave Fisher's life, 59

Oh, young Lochinvar is come out of the West, 93
Open to me thy heart of heart's deep core, 113
OUT IN THE FIELDS WITH GOD, 95

PATRIOTISM, 75
PRACTICE OF THE PRESENCE OF GOD, THE, 58, 96
Praise the Lord! 20
Put in the plow, 72
Put thy trust in God, 72

RAIN IS OVER AND GONE, THE, 110
REASONS FOR CONSTANCY, 169
REMEMBER THESE WORDS, 184
ROMEO AND JULIET, 88

Say over again, and yet once over again, 114
SHE DWELT AMONG THE UNTRODDEN WAYS, 18
She sweeps with many-colored brooms, 110
SILAS MARNER, 140
SILENT NOON, 107
SIR GALAHAD, 104
So let us love, dear love, live as we ought, 25
SOMEBODY LOVES YOU, 102
SOMEBODY LOVES YOU, more than you know, 102
SONNET OF CONTENTMENT, 56
Speak low to me, my Saviour, low and sweet, 101
STATE OF BLESSEDNESS, A, 61
Such is the patriot's boast, where'er we roam, 74
SURRENDER, 44

TALE OF TWO CITIES, A, 117
That I did always love, 185
The best portion of a good man's life, 99
The Cock is crowing, 110
The essence of all beauty, I call love, 108
The first time that the sun rose on thine oath, 117

The heart hath its own memory, like the mind, 18
The little cares that fretted me, 95
The Lord is my shepherd, I shall not want, 98
The Lord is the portion of mine inheritance and of my cup, 73
The quality of mercy is not strained, 70
There is no time like the old time, when you and I were young, 19
There was a man with a tongue of wood, 114
Therefore the Lord himself shall give you a sign, 65
There's a wideness in God's mercy, 70
TIME LONG PAST, 17
TO A BIRD AFTER A STORM, 21
TO KEEP A TRUE LENT, 63
To one who has been long in city pent, 56
To these whom death again did wed, 185

UNFADING BEAUTY, THE, 108

We are gathered together, 184
WHAT IS LOVE? 188
What secret trouble stirs thy heart? 96
What we behold is censured by our eyes, 84
When I have seen by Time's fell hand defaced, 134
When, in disgrace with fortune and men's eyes, 170
WHEN LOVE IS KIND, 100
When music spills from golden throat, 97
When thou turn'st away from ill, 174
Where did you come from, baby dear, 54
WISH OF DIOGENES, THE, 75
WITH GOD AS YOUR PARTNER, 50

YOU SAY I LOVE NOT, 89
You say I love not, 'cause I do not play, 89
Your hands lie open in the long fresh grass, 107

AUTHORS

Addison, Joseph, 26, 174
Alcott, Louisa M., 35
Allen, James, 61, 115, 173

Bonar, Horatius, 183
Brooks, Phillips, 115
Browning, Elizabeth Barrett, 31, 92, 101, 108, 109, 114, 117, 173
Browning, Robert, 57, 72, 175
Bunyan, John, 57, 76
Burns, Robert, 74
Byron, George Gordon, 133, 168

Carew, Thomas, 108
Carlyle, Thomas, 161
Chekhov, Anton, 135
Cowper, William, 109
Crane, Stephen, 114
Crashaw, Richard, 185

Dickens, Charles, 62, 117, 159
Dickinson, Emily, 25, 110, 159, 185
Donne, John, 32, 68, 90
Dostoevski, Feodor, 175
Dryden, John, 76

Eliot, George, 113, 140, 161
Emerson, Ralph Waldo, 25, 26, 43, 92, 97, 169

Epicurus, 26, 96

Faber, Frederick W., 70
Franklin, Benjamin, 29, 99
Freneau, Philip, 75

Goethe, Johann Wolfgang von, 90, 113
Goldsmith, Oliver, 74
Graham, Billy, 190

Herbert, George, 65, 99
Herrick, Robert, 63, 89
Holmes, Marjorie, 91
Holmes, Oliver Wendell, 19, 27, 113
Hugo, Victor, 18, 29
Hunt, Leigh, 160, 161, 186

Jefferson, Thomas, 72
Johnson, Samuel, 25
Jowett, John Henry, 103

Keats, John, 56, 160

La Rochefoucauld, 90
Lanier, Sidney, 69, 116
Lawrence, Brother, 22, 58, 96
Lazarus, Emma, 101
Lee, Robert E., 53
Lincoln, A., 28
Longfellow, Henry Wadsworth, 13, 18, 73, 83, 96, 173

Lowell, James Russell, 30

MacArthur, General Douglas A., 116
MacDonald, George, 44, 54, 174
Marlowe, Christopher, 84
Marshall, Catherine, 14
Martial, 18
Maupassant, Guy de, 170
Mead, Frank S., 77
Moore, Thomas, 100

Newton, John, 183

Patrick, Saint, 188
Peale, Norman Vincent, 175
Plato, 13
Poe, Edgar Allan, 87, 107
Price, Eugenia, 161

Quarles, Francis, 23

Rice, Helen Steiner, 21, 50, 102, 184, 188
Rossetti, Christina, 64, 89, 97
Rossetti, Dante Gabriel, 107
Rostand, Edmond, 84
Ruskin, John, 62

Schurz, Carl, 30

Scott, Sir Walter, 26, 75, 93
Sedley, Sir Charles, 169
Seneca, 26
Shakespeare, William, 27, 70, 88, 134, 170
Shelley, Percy Bysshe, 17
Sidney, Sir Philip, 112
Spenser, Edmund, 25
Stevenson, Robert Louis, 13, 49
Stowe, Harriet Beecher, 29, 55, 109
Swift, Jonathan, 69

Tennyson, Alfred, 53, 104
Thackeray, William Makepeace, 54, 57, 113
Thomas à Kempis, 30, 72
Thoreau, Henry David, 111, 113, 115
Tolstoy, Leo, 29, 45, 66
Trench, Archbishop Richard Chenevix, 22

Vaughan, Henry, 21

Walton, Izaak, 59
Wesley, Charles, 186, 190
Whitman, Walt, 24, 25, 109
Whittier, John Greenleaf, 103, 108
Wordsworth, William, 18, 22, 25, 99, 110